The Mathematics Curriculum

NUMBER

The Mathematics Curriculum: A Critical Review
was a project set up by the Schools Council at the University of Nottingham 1973–77

Members of the central project team were

Professor J. V. Armitage (Principal, College of St. Hild
and St. Bede, Durham), Director
Professor H. Halberstam (Department of Mathematics,
University of Nottingham), Co-Director (1975–77)
Mr. G. R. H. Boys (1973–76)
Mrs. J. A. Gadsden
Dr. R. B. Coates (1973–74)

The books in this series are

Geometry
From Graphs to Calculus
Mathematics across the Curriculum
Number
Algebra
Counting and Configurations
Mathematics in the World
Eleven to Thirteen

The Mathematics Curriculum

NUMBER

Written for the Project by
JOHN HUNTER and MARTYN CUNDY

Published for the Schools Council by BLACKIE

ISBN 0 216 90338 6

First published 1978

Copyright © 1978 Schools Council Publications

Illustrator: Julie Gadsden

Published by Blackie and Son Limited, Bishopbriggs, Glasgow;
and 450/452 Edgware Road, London W2 1EG

Printed in Great Britain by Thomson Litho Ltd., East Kilbride, Scotland

Preface

This book is one of a series produced by the Schools Council Project: *The Mathematics Curriculum—A Critical Review*. This Project was initiated by the Mathematics Committee of the Schools Council as a result of letters received from teachers asking for guidance on the vast amount of new mathematical literature which had been produced for schools during the 1960s. The Project was set up in 1973 and was based at the Shell Centre for Mathematical Education at Nottingham University.

It was felt that teachers, who faced a daunting array of mathematical literature and novel classroom material, would welcome a basis for constructive and critical discussion of the content of the school mathematics curriculum. Moreover, whilst the choice of syllabus, books, materials, methods and presentation belonged properly to the teacher, the range of choices was so vast as to make well-informed decisions consistent with professional integrity well nigh impossible; so that any advice implicit in these books, far from detracting from the teachers' role, would rather establish it.

The fundamental aim of the Project, therefore, is to help teachers to perform their own critical appraisal of existing mathematics syllabuses and teaching apparatus for secondary school pupils in the 11 to 16 age range, with the objective of making, for them, optimal choices. Such an aim, however fundamental it may be, is still inadequate. It was never the intention of those responsible for the Project that they should provide only a review of mathematical literature and apparatus, for an exercise of that kind would be obsolescent before the material could be published. Instead, the Project was conceived as a contribution both to initial and to post-experience in-service training, as well as providing helpful private reading.

Although the Project was not intended to be an exercise in curriculum development, it was almost inevitable and certainly desirable that a review of existing syllabuses should lead to a consideration of the possibility of a synthesis of "modern" and "traditional". I believe that such a synthesis is possible and, indeed, sorely needed. So, although we have not attempted to spell out an optimum syllabus, we have tried to identify the important ideas and skills which should be represented at school, and to show how so-called modern and traditional topics are related. We hope that one of the lessons which emerges from these books is that the two can be integrated in a unified presentation of mathematics and its applications. Perhaps the current numeracy debate will lead to syllabus revision. If so, it must be informed by sound mathematical and pedagogical considerations, to which end these books are devoted.

In order to focus as wide a range of experience as possible on the task, planning teams were established, each under the chairmanship of a potential author (an Editorial Fellow) and comprising representatives from Universities, Polytechnics, Colleges of Education, Schools, the Inspectorate and the Advisory Services. The material produced was referred to working groups of teachers across the country—from Cornwall and the Channel Islands to Northumberland. Moreover, the groups were invited to make original contributions as well as to comment on planning material. All the material thus made available was then referred once more to the original planning team, who now assume responsibility for advising the Editorial Fellow on the "final" write-up, which in some cases received further redaction by other writers. The result is now before the reader.

The dictionary definition of mathematics as "the science of space and number" is still arguably the most appropriate and, from the outset, the books on geometry and on number have been regarded as fundamental to the rest of the Project.

Hardy and Wright proposed at one time to call their classic not *An Introduction to the Theory of Numbers* but rather *An Introduction to Arithmetic*. The change arose from the possible confusion and misunderstanding as to the contents which the latter might cause. To a mathematician, arithmetic means number theory: the systematic study of the natural number system and related questions, which was monumentally established by Gauss in his *Disquisitiones Arithmeticae* (1801) and which has been the favourite study of the greatest mathematicians as well as of many amateurs. But in popular usage arithmetic represents a deposit of more or less useful computational skills which are supposed (erroneously) at one time to have been the common possession of school leavers and whose acquisition is still (rightly) considered to be desirable.

The theme of this book is that arithmetic in both senses should be a part of the experience of pupils at school and that an encounter with one of the most sublime achievements of the human spirit is by no means incompatible with the acquisition of desirable skills. Moreover, just as training for an athletic event is frequently set in the context of a varied training programme, so also numeracy is best developed in the rich context of number theory.

J. V. Armitage

Acknowledgements

The authors wish to thank the many people who have contributed to the writing of this book. The planning team played a particularly important part; its members were:

Mr J. Anthony (Glasgow Academy)

Mr M. N. Edwards (Mathematics Adviser, Leicestershire)

Mr D. S. Fielker (Abbey Wood Mathematics Centre)

Mr D. S. Hale (H.M.I.)

Mr E. Harper (School of Education, University of Bath)

Mrs T. H. Marklew (Archbishop Williams School, Birmingham)

Mr D. Wheatley (Margaret Glen-Bott School, Nottingham)

The contributions of Dr M. Stevens (Tulse Hill School), Professor H. Halberstam (Department of Mathematics, University of Nottingham), and Dr T. J. Fletcher (H.M.I.) were constructive and valuable, as also were the comments and criticisms received from working groups of teachers in Liverpool, Cheshire, Durham, East London, Bristol, Guernsey, York, Coventry, and Cheltenham.

Contents

In Praise of Arithmetic
by Professor H. Halberstam

Arithmetic and geometry are the two oldest branches of mathematics. Born of necessity, each has also occupied, since earliest times, a special place in the human imagination; geometry because of its beauty and arithmetic by virtue of its mystery. Both provide essential tools for our understanding of physical reality, and their inexhaustible riches inspire and sustain the growth of mathematics.

The mysteries of arithmetic derive from the opacity of numbers. Write down a ten-digit integer, and there is little or nothing we learn, by casual inspection, of its multiplicative or additive structure. Is it a prime or not? If composite, what are the factors; how many are there; what, for example, is the relationship between the sum of its divisors and the number itself; can it be written as the sum of a small number of squares, or cubes, or fourth powers, etc., and in how many ways; is it a sum of primes? Little wonder that certain numbers acquired magical status in ancient times; the fact that we still know so little about deficient, perfect, abundant and amicable numbers indicates the depth of these earliest arithmetical perceptions.

The propositions of arithmetic are practically never intuitively obvious. Even such simple results as

$$1 + 3 + 5 + \ldots + (2n - 1) = n^2$$

or

$$1^3 + 2^3 + 3^3 + \ldots + n^3 = (1 + 2 + 3 + \ldots + n)^2$$

surprise us; not only do we feel the need to justify these results—are they *really* true for *all* natural numbers n?—but our curiosity is aroused. Is it true that

$$7 \text{ divides into } 5555^{2222} + 2222^{5555}$$

and why? We are rightly reluctant to check by first multiplying out! Is there an underlying pattern here? (See chapter 10, p. 115 for a solution of this problem.)

Consider the following set of calculations:

$$1 \times 9 + 2 = 11$$
$$12 \times 9 + 3 = 111$$
$$123 \times 9 + 4 = 1111$$
$$1234 \times 9 + 5 = 11111$$
$$12345 \times 9 + 6 = 111111$$
$$123456 \times 9 + 7 = 1111111$$
$$1234567 \times 9 + 8 = 11111111$$
$$12345678 \times 9 + 9 = 111111111$$

First of all, is it correct? If correct, what is the explanation? Can you find other such designs of "sums"? As some of the later chapters show, the possibilities for uncovering number patterns are limitless, and in all of them are present two key aspects of all scientific activity: the need to experiment and the intellectual compulsion to prove.

The place of arithmetic in contemporary school mathematics is so uncertain that it may be helpful to begin with the question: what *is* arithmetic? The Greeks distinguished between two branches of the subject: *logistica* or the study of *reckoning*, and *arithmetica* or the study of *numbers*; and in time a third branch came to be recognized, *logistica speciosa* (as Vieta called it) or *symbolic method*—or *algebra* as it was called until the early years of the nineteenth century among professionals and until the advent of the "new mathematics" in schools: the use of contracted notation and of letters for numbers as an aid to solving problems. In my view these are still the three principal headings under which to organize the teaching of arithmetic:

(a) the study of reckoning,

(b) the study of number,

(c) the study of method.

Of course, these should not be considered in terms of water-tight compartmentation—on the contrary, work under each heading can reinforce, and be enriched by, work in the others.

RECKONING

In the *study of reckoning* we may distinguish four components:

  (i) the representation of numbers,

  (ii) computing skills,

  (iii) the number system,

  (iv) mechanical aids to computation.

The four are interdependent and the order in which they are written should not be taken to imply a logical sequence—historically they developed if anything in reverse order, and in a successful programme of instruction we would expect to see all four interwoven. For example, even at the earliest stage of learning, Cuisenaire rods serve as concrete representations of small integers; we may use them to discover some of the basic laws of arithmetic, and at the same time children will learn to use them as a device for arriving speedily at answers to sums. Nevertheless, each of the four components encountered profound difficulties in its development, and the conquest of these is a significant portion of our cultural heritage, as much a part of history as the record of national conflicts or of the socio-economic evolution of society.

The decimal system of representing numbers stands at the end of two millenia of painfully slow growth; we should make some mention of this when introducing it to children. In mediaeval times its use was commonly regarded as an occult practice; it did not come into general use until the sixteenth century, and the first systematic account of decimal fractions, by Simon Stevin, did not appear until 1585. What are the virtues of the decimal system? First of all—and this is vital—it made possible the execution of complicated calculations. The following story, dating from the sixteenth century, illustrates both awareness of the problem and the importance then attached to it:

> A certain German merchant had a son to whom he desired to give an advanced commercial education. He appealed to a prominent university professor for advice as to where he should send his son. The reply was that if the mathematical curriculum of the young man was to be confined to adding and subtracting, he could perhaps obtain instruction in a German university; but the art of multiplying and dividing, he continued, had been greatly developed in Italy, which in his opinion was the only country where such advanced instruction could be obtained.

And, indeed, the dramatic increase at that time in the scale and complexity of both scientific and commercial activity made it essential to be able to carry out all these operations, and others, with accuracy and reasonable speed. The sense of achievement was great. A measure of it is the fervour with which the arts of long multiplication and division—and of extracting square roots—have been expounded in school for four hundred years, until recently; and children can still feel afresh a sense of achievement when they learn to master these arts, and their love of repetition—a whole page of sums of the same kind, so much an object of scorn nowadays—is, in fact, an unconscious tribute to this epic triumph. At a more sophisticated level, but still in the same direction, is the compilation of mathematical tables of all kinds; and underlying these, of course, is the notion of *systematic* approximation of complicated quantities—the irrationals for example, or even fractions, like

$$\frac{57017951}{710920033}$$

of which the approximation

$$0{\cdot}080203044440$$

is much more illuminating. There is also the estimation of *large* numbers in terms of orders of magnitude; in some contexts it is, for example, more helpful to think of

$$610790057917$$

as being of order of magnitude 6×10^{11}. The representation of numbers using other number bases can be valuable as a pedagogic device, and at some stage it is important to point to problem situations where a particular number base is mathematically appropriate to the structure of the problem—there are many illustrations in which the binary system should be used, e.g. the game of Nim[1]; and the counterfeit-coin problem[2] is an example where use of the ternary system reveals the underlying structure— but excessive computation using other number bases, virtually for its own sake, is to be discouraged.

The classification of numbers, and the structure of the number system, are topics fraught with difficulty at all levels of instruction. While a normal child nowadays will accept the natural numbers as a *natural* abstraction of his experiences with counting and ordering, each subsequent enlargement of the number system, i.e. the successive adjunction of 0, the negative integers, the rationals, the irrationals and the complex numbers, represents a conceptual threshold and should be explained in practical contexts of men creating new kinds of numbers to explain new situations or solve new problems. That is how it happened, and if we study old mathematical texts we see again and again mathematicians using new kinds of numbers even as they voice "theological" doubts as to their existence.

The positive rational numbers already confront us as teachers with problems. Here we cannot count on the child to have himself carried out the process of abstraction, nor to have accepted as natural the means of adding and multiplying fractions. Instead, we have to implant in the child's mind some useful model of the number system (e.g. the geometrical model in which numbers are

represented by lengths) in which the rationals and operations with them make good sense. It is instructive to remember that the Egyptians used, with few exceptions, only the reciprocals of integers as rational numbers (i.e. fractions with numerator 1), and that the Greeks took over the Egyptian system of computation, with the consequence that we find various Greek mathematicians *compiling tables* for calculations involving rational numbers. If we do remember, then we shall not be quite so surprised that many adults cannot recall how to evaluate $2\frac{1}{2} \times 3\frac{2}{5}$, even though they may claim that they were "very good at it" at school!

Remember the panic of the Pythagoreans when they discovered the incommensurability of the hypotenuse of the right-angled triangle with the other two sides of length 1. Even a thousand years later the commentator Proclus could write:

> It is told that those who first brought out the irrationals from concealment into the open perished in a shipwreck, to a man. For the unutterable and the formless must each be concealed. And those who uncovered and touched this image of life were instantly destroyed and shall remain forever exposed to the play of the external waves.

Yet, notwithstanding this terror of irrational quantities—and we might here remember also the use of the word "irrational" in everyday language—Eudoxus' theory of ratio (expounded in Book V of Euclid and the mathematical pinnacle of that work) gave a wholly satisfactory account of irrational quantities in the context of geometrical magnitudes; and Eudoxus was driven to this because he saw that even the basic properties of similar triangles could not be established satisfactorily without it.

It is not hard to see why a child might regard the need for irrationals with incredulity. If we mark off on an interval of length 1—with a beautifully sharpened pencil—the point $\frac{1}{2}$, then $\frac{1}{3}$ and $\frac{2}{3}$, then $\frac{1}{4}$ and $\frac{3}{4}$, then $\frac{1}{5}, \frac{2}{5}, \frac{3}{5}, \frac{4}{5}$, etc., we shall soon appear to be "filling in" the whole interval; and we cannot but be astounded to learn that, despite this "experiment", and even if we had been physically able to mark off *all* fractions in this way, we should still have failed

[1] *Mathematical Puzzles and Diversions*, Martin Gardner, Pelican, 1965, Chapter 15.
[2] *The Gentle Art of Mathematics*, Dan Pedoe, Pelican, 1963, p. 30.

to mark off some points on the line. Indeed, the work of Cantor shows that we should actually have failed to mark off most of the points between 0 and 1! While Cantor's argument is too difficult for the age range considered in this series of books, it is not hard to prove that, in the above procedure, we are bound to miss out $1/\sqrt{2}$—for if, on the contrary, there exist integers such that $m/n = 1/\sqrt{2}$, then $2m^2 = n^2$. This cannot be true because a squared integer has an even number of prime factors; and so the number of prime factors of n^2 is even, while the number of prime factors of $2m^2$ is odd—and, by the Fundamental Theorem of Arithmetic, an integer cannot have (ordering apart) two different factorizations into primes.

Showing the need for the real (or complex) number systems is one thing, showing how to build it up, stage by stage, is quite another! Hamilton considered the complex numbers as ordered pairs of reals; then Dedekind used the method of Eudoxus to construct the reals from the rationals; and last of all came the method of building the integers from the natural numbers, and the rationals from the integers (again using the idea of ordered pairs). While every teacher of mathematics should have some appreciation of this process of construction—for one thing, every teacher should be prepared to find brilliant children in his class who ask genuinely difficult questions—it is doubtful whether the process itself should be taught formally as part of a school course. Even in universities it is avoided nowadays by simply postulating the real-number and complex-number systems as having certain structural properties; and this procedure is successful so long as the students have enough varied experience with numbers of all kinds to recognize in the postulated system all the features they expect. Is it unreasonable to expect most of our 16-year-old school leavers to see the positive real numbers as the set of all numbers of type

$$n + 0 \cdot a_1 a_2 a_3 \ldots (0 \leqslant a_i \leqslant 9)$$

where n is a non-negative integer, to know how to add and multiply them, to know when one such number is bigger than another, and to identify the rationals as precisely those numbers whose decimal expansions are either terminating or recurring? Of course, the notion of an infinite decimal is not easy; but the interpretation of $0 \cdot a_1 a_2 \ldots$ as a sequence of "geographical" directions towards the precise location of the number on the number-line is not only acceptable but actually helpful. Also, the idea of an infinite process (and of finite approximations to it) is so basic in mathematics that we may as well encounter it early and have lots of time to reflect on it.

Artificial aids to fast computation are of ancient origin. Finger counting, the abacus and various kinds of counting board are early examples, and experts in the use of these devices are capable of astonishing calculating speeds. Napier discovered his famous "rods" in 1613, the slide rule was devised between 1630 and 1633 by Delamain and Oughtred, and the first mechanical calculating machine was constructed as long ago as 1642 by Pascal; and now we have pocket electronic computers at no more than the price of a good slide rule. It is interesting that, while slide rules have been available for so many years now, they have never been seen as a cause for substantial change in the teaching of arithmetic; yet now it is widely believed that pocket calculators must revolutionize it. What is quite certain is that these calculators offer a wonderful opportunity to display successive approximation procedures and convergence phenomena in a way that will lend a completely new degree of conviction to work that has always been regarded hitherto as conceptually difficult (see the detailed discussion in chapter 8).

NUMBER

In the *study of number*—or "the higher arithmetic" as Gauss called it—we concern ourselves for the most part with questions about the structure of numbers or number sequences which, by their nature, cannot be answered, even in principle, solely by means of numerical computation. Just consider the following statements:

(1) There exist infinitely many primes.

(2) For every prime p, $(p-1)!+1$ is divisible by p.

(3) Every natural number is the sum of one, two, three or four squares of positive integers.

(4) Every even natural number $n > 4$ is the sum of two odd primes.

(5) Given an irrational number θ, there exist infinitely many distinct rationals m/n such that $|\theta - m/n| < 1/n^2$.

(6) π is irrational.

(7) On average, a natural number n has about $\log_e n$ positive integer divisors.

(8) Almost all natural numbers n have about $\log_e \log_e n$ prime divisors.

(9) The equation $x^m - y^n = 1$ has no solutions in integers $x > 1, y > 1, m > 1, n > 1$ other than $x = n = 3, y = m = 2$.

(10) For each integer $n \geqslant 3$, the equation $x^n + y^n = z^n$ has no solution in non-zero integers x, y, z.

(11) For each integer $n \geqslant 2$, there is at least one prime between n^2 and $(n+1)^2$.

(12) There exist infinitely many integers n such that $n^2 + 1$ is a prime.

(13) For every prime p, $n^p - n$ is divisible by p for every integer n.

(14) For every positive integer $n > 3$, there are, among the odd primes not exceeding n, more of the form $4k+3$ than of the form $4k+1$.

(15) If $n = a_r 10^{r-1} + a_{r-1} 10^{r-2} + \ldots + a_1$, then 3 is a factor of n if and only if 3 divides $a_r + a_{r-1} + \ldots + a_1$.

(16) In modular arithmetic to prime modulus p, there exists an integer g such that $1, g, g^2 \ldots, g^{p-2}$ are, modulo p, equal to $1, 2, \ldots, p-1$ in some order.

While several of these statements were first conjectured on the basis of experimental evidence, and experimental evidence strongly supports belief in the truth of several others, there is not a single one where numerical computation alone can lead to a proof. In the case of (4), for instance, numerical evidence suggests not only that it is true, but even that each even n has many representations of the kind stated, yet we still do not know whether (4) is true or not. Similarly (10)—Fermat's notorious "last theorem"—has been proved for many values of n, and much of modern algebra has sprung from attempts to settle the question, but still we do not know even that there exist infinitely many prime values of n for which (10) is true. As for (14), experimental evidence strongly supported belief in its truth, but J. E. Littlewood actually disproved it—not by exhibiting an n for which (14) fails, but by showing that the statement fails infinitely often! In the case of (9) we know from the recent work of R. Tijdeman and A. Baker that only finitely many solutions can exist, and we even have explicit bounds for these possible solutions; but the bounds are so huge that a straightforward computer check is out of the question.

We have therefore in arithmetic a marvellous opportunity to see how a science evolves: from observation to conjecture, from conjecture to experimentation, perhaps back again to a modified conjecture, then in the end, sometimes to a theorem or even a general theory. Pencil and paper are the only scientific equipment required, and quite innocent perceptions may lead to profoundly difficult problems—I met a beautiful illustration of this recently. A colleague has three sons, one of whom remarked that this year the ages of father and sons were all prime numbers: 7, 11, 13 and 47. He asked his father whether this would happen again. Of course, the answer is simple here: in six years' time, because 13, 17, 19 and 53 are also all primes. But the same question might be asked again then, and at the next occurrence, and so on. As one goes on, such prime "quadruplets" are increasingly hard to find—and to check—but if one were to discuss this problem in class, one might find someone asking sooner or later, in so many words: are there infinitely many prime quadruples of the type

$$p, p+4, p+6, p+40?$$

The class would then have been taken right to the edge of the unknown, for we still do not know the answer—we suspect that it is "yes", but the proof at present seems utterly out of reach. Nevertheless, a class might still do some useful things in this context. For example, it is not possible for $p, p+2, p+4$ all to be primes if $p > 3$, since $(p+2)(p+4) = p^2 + 6p + 8 = (p^2 - 1) + 6p + 9$ is divisible by 3 for all primes $p > 3$. So one might ask more generally, for other pairs of integers a, b, which are ruled out if $p, p+a, p+b$ is to be a prime triple?

Perhaps we should add that, of the 16 statements at the beginning of this section, most are very difficult; but there is every reason why statements (1), (2), (13), (15) and (16) should be part of every child's arithmetical experience, and there are several items, e.g. (3) and (5), which could form the basis of valuable class-room activity. Statement (3) could be used to illustrate the importance of algebraic identities—a number that is the product of two numbers which are sums of two (four) squares is itself the product of two (four) squares; and statement (5) could be used to discuss the approximation of irrational by rational numbers. The decimal representation of numbers obviously affords one standard procedure of successive approximation, but (5) indicates that there exists a much more efficient method of approximation (actually, by means of continued fractions). Kronecker once compared those who concern themselves with the higher arithmetic to lotus-eaters who "once having consumed this food can never give it up". Should not our children have the opportunity to develop this particular appetite?

NUMERACY AND PROBLEM-SOLVING

Little has been said so far about the *practical* uses of arithmetic—about basic numeracy and the arithmetic of con-temporary citizenship. Such uses arise in the problem situations of everyday working life *and* in leisure occupations. As we shop, cook, paper our walls, put up shelves, use our wages, do our football pools, measure out dosages, plan investments, play darts, study cricket averages, discuss the budget, read maps, plan car journeys, check the gas bill, stock-take, order goods, etc., we require familiarity with arithmetic; without it, all but the most menial forms of employment are closed to us, and much of day-to-day life is frustrating, bewildering and even meaningless. In our technological society, with its stress on planning, efficiency and optimization, novel applications of mathematics abound, as they do both in the sciences of engineering, genetics and meteorology and in subjects like economics, anthropology and linguistics; in all these applications a sophisticated number sense is essential. To do our job, to enjoy our leisure and to follow events, we must all be numerate. It has been said, with some justice, that we are witnessing in the present age the mathematization of all human knowledge; it is more important than ever before to provide children with a firm and durable mathematical foundation.

Every child solves problems of one kind or another, both real and artificial, from his earliest days in the cradle, and his experience, reinforced by legend and fairy tale (ancient or modern), must be that nature speaks to us in riddles. At the same time as we recognize that problems are in the nature of things, we have to admit too that problems can be frightening. Much is made of the fear that mathematics inspires in children—and adults—and there is an implication that bad teaching is to blame. It is preferable to think of fear in this situation, as in crossing a road, as a normal reaction; a child learns how to cross the road by following a certain discipline of sensible procedures in response to what he observes— and so too, faced with a mathematical problem, we may learn to overcome initial panic ("I don't even know how to start") by disciplined reflection. In both cases the issue is rather one of acquiring good habits.

We expect arithmetic in schools to reflect in significant measure the problem situations of "real" life. The repertoire of arithmetical problems suitable for the classroom has certainly been greatly enriched in our time from practical sources such as statistics, flow charts, computers, coding, combinatorial arithmetic, linear programming, critical path analysis, etc. We do have to realize, however, that relevance must, inevitably, be circumscribed by the limitation of children's knowledge of technique, of other branches of mathematics and even (*pace* interdisciplinary studies) of other subjects. We have to simplify "reality", often to such an extent that the problems come to look artificial or down-right fanciful. Actually, this should not worry us—and if it does not, it will certainly not worry the children; for in simplifying real situations we teach children the basic procedure of applied mathematics: to mirror reality in terms of models that, on the one hand, reflect some important features of reality and, on the other, are simple enough for us to study effectively.

Take the following problem, which is transcribed* from the so-called *Greek Anthology* of the fifth century A.D. but, no doubt, is much older:

> Water runs into a tank from four pipes. The water coming from one pipe would fill the tank in a day, that from the second would fill it in two days, that from the third in three days, and that from the fourth in four days. How long will it take to fill the tank if water flows in from all four pipes together?

Every teacher will recognize this problem, and may well regard it as boring and in no sense representative of the mathematics of the jet age. Nevertheless, it is a perfectly sensible, real question. To state the solution succinctly, pipe n on its own fills in one day $\frac{1}{n}$-th of the tank ($n = 1, 2, 3, 4$); all four together therefore would fill in one day $1 + \frac{1}{2} + \frac{1}{3} + \frac{1}{4} = \frac{25}{12}$ tanks of the same size. Hence they fill the one tank in $\frac{12}{25}$ths, or just less than half of a day.

* P. Dedron and J. Itard, *Mathematics and Mathematicians, Vol. 2*, Transworld Publishers Ltd. (1974).

Here is the same problem, made relevant to sixteenth-century Venice:

> A ship is equipped with three sails. With the largest it can make a certain voyage in two days. With the medium-sized sail the voyage takes three days, and with the smallest sail four days. How many days would it take if all the sails were used at once?

The question is now more exciting for the children of a seafaring nation. The same method of solution is called for, but now there are physical aspects of the new situation which, implicitly, are to be suppressed; and the answer will no longer reflect the full reality.

It would be a fascinating piece of scholarship to prepare an anthology of problems from all extant arithmetical texts. As is indicated in the book cited, we should find many problems coming up again and again, often in a variety of quasi-real guises reflecting what different ages deemed relevant; and we should then become less impatient with the problems we have come to regard as "hackneyed". I well remember a distinguished industrialist telling me how the hoary old "leaking bath" problem had turned up not so long ago, in a different guise, in his electronics laboratory!

Broadly speaking, school problems in arithmetic fall into three developmental stages. First come the problems which amount to little more than straightforward description. Here, in response to questions such as "how much", "how far", "how long", "how large", "in which order" and "where", we learn to quantify in terms of simple numbers and elementary operations with them. We might venture the definition that having the skills to cope readily with this category of problem constitutes basic numeracy. Next come those problems in which the same questions may be asked, but the solutions involve some systematic analysis followed by a standard arithmetical routine (such as solving a simple equation, or a pair of simultaneous equations). In this category of problem the power of mathematical method becomes manifest—to reduce an apparently complicated statement to, for example, a simple equation should be an exhilarating experience. Here, too, we may look for opportunities to generalize, and to develop notation. Finally, there are the problems where systematic and routine skills may need to be allied to some spark of originality—an insight or intuition. These latter problems are chiefly for the abler children, although often the less able too can derive profit and pleasure from them by experimentation, because it is important for them to learn that, while routines are crucial in mathematics, not all of mathematics is routine; indeed, that the scope for originality in mathematics is without limit. (Too many people, even among the highly educated, ask: but how is it possible to do research in mathematics?)

There is no royal road to problem-solving, but there are a few sensible general rules that should emerge from classroom discussion and the accumulation of experience. The first rule—a golden one, surely—is to study the statement of the problem *carefully and without prejudice*. It is vital to recognize the pertinent data, to identify what is unknown, and to set all this down as simply as possible by stripping off everything that is inessential. I say "without prejudice" because it is all too tempting to jump to premature conclusions; we see a few familiar words or phrases and, without reading the question properly, say, "Ah yes, I remember questions like that; what you do is…" and promptly enter upon some familiar arithmetical routine without checking properly that it is appropriate. I caught myself doing this with the following problem (also from the *Greek Anthology* quoted earlier):

> "Tell me, learned Pythagoras, how many pupils come to your school and listen to your teachings?"
> "Well," replied the Philosopher, "half of them study mathematics, a quarter study music, a seventh of them keep silence, and there are also three women."

Without hesitation I let x be the number of pupils, wrote down the equation

$$x = \tfrac{1}{2}x + \tfrac{1}{4}x + \tfrac{1}{7}x + 3$$

and got the answer $x = 28$. Then I looked again and saw that my argument must be nonsense. Even assuming that the groups studying mathematics, music and remaining silent are mutually exclusive, the three women must be distributed among these groups, and then the equation is wrong; or they form a fourth group, in which case the equation is wrong again, since then only men are involved in the first three groups. Instead I argued as follows: x is a rational number as are $\tfrac{1}{2}x$, $\tfrac{1}{4}x$ and $\tfrac{1}{7}x$. Hence x is a multiple of 28, the least rational number divisible by 2, 4 and 7; the information about the three women present tells us nothing about which the multiple of 28 is at stake and yet, since Pythagoras gives no further information, we must presume that his listeners would know that higher multiples of 28, i.e. 56 or 84, etc., are out of the question. Hence 28 is the answer again: 25 men and three women. Note that in this argument I have not had to assume that the three groups are disjoint.*

So, as Polya enjoins, *first understand your problem*. Next, *formulate the problem* in numerical terms as simply and suggestively as possible, bearing carefully in mind what operations and relations between the quantities involved are appropriate. This stage should reveal whether the given data are sufficient—it can easily happen, especially in "real life" situations, that the given information is inadequate or, on the other hand, that an excess of information is provided. The little problem just described illustrates this second rule. At the first attempt I formulated the problem as a simple equation; and this would have been correct if there had been four disjoint groups of students, the last group of three pupils studying philosophy, say. The fact that $\tfrac{1}{2}x$, $\tfrac{1}{4}x$ and $\tfrac{1}{7}x$

---

* Editorial Footnote. There are two other possible interpretations of this problem.
(a) It may be a subtle jest, the author implying that women can neither be serious students, nor can they keep silence, so they are necessarily distinct from the earlier groups.
(b) The Greek, however, is against this, because it adds "…three women, of whom Theano is the best"; the women therefore were students at least capable of being assessed. Since, however, all the fractional adjectives used earlier appear (in the Greek) in the masculine form, we are probably to assume that they refer to male students, and the first solution would have been expected. But no doubt Pythagoras would have been pleased with the foregoing.

are integers was not used explicitly, but came out, as it were, "in the wash". In the second attempt, on the contrary, seizing on this arithmetic aspect, we saw that the number of women present was irrelevant, and had to interpolate additional evidence, such as might have been supplied by Pythagoras saying, for instance, "Also, I never take more than 50 pupils".

At the third stage—and this is hardly a rule—we attempt to solve the problem which, in our context, will often amount to solving an equation or set of equations, or a set of inequalities. As problems grow more difficult, various complicating factors enter the scene. It may be necessary, for example, to introduce intermediate quantities which do not feature in the statement of the problem but are needed for the formulation. Or it may be necessary to have a grasp of non-elementary concepts such as rate of change of one quantity with another, or proportionality; these can be troublesome, for the notion of functionality is implicit in both and, also, a child with a poor sense of number may have difficulty in knowing what to make, say, of dividing a number of metres by a number of seconds. At the stage of solution an important component is to be distinguished: interpreting one's answer and checking it. For example, solving the equation may produce several "answers", only one of which should be relevant; also we might consider the answer in the light of the original question, to judge whether it is reasonable.

Ideally, children should be taken through initial attempts at problem-solving slowly and informally; they should be encouraged to compare and discuss their ideas under careful guidance, so that they realize the need to become mathematically articulate and, almost unconsciously, themselves arrive at various simplifying devices and notations which are so important in mathematics. Good notation is no more than a contracted form of ordinary language, but is so well adapted to the thinking process that often it bears within itself, by automatic suggestion, the seeds of further progress. On the other hand, some notational devices used by professionals as time-savers (such as implication signs, $\exists$, $\forall$) confuse children, and it is all too obvious from the use of them by university students that they are imperfectly understood. Later, children should be encouraged to generalize, i.e. to see that solutions of certain problems stated with specific numbers can also be stated much more generally, so that a whole class of problems can be solved in one "go". Here we encounter the use of letters as generalized numbers, and children should feel the sense of new power this bestows on them.

Later still children should encounter problems that are out of the common pattern, where past experience is of relatively little avail except as a source of confidence. Here we should encounter the need for insight—to seize on an illuminating formulation of the problem (there are often several) or on the critical feature. Let us look at two illustrations:

(i) Given an $8'' \times 8''$ rectangular grid of squares of side $1''$, with two opposite corner squares removed, and a large supply of $1'' \times 2''$ rectangular counters, can one cover the "trimmed" grid completely with the counters but without overlap?

An illuminating formulation is *to think of the grid as a chequer-board* of alternatively black and white squares, and of each counter as covering one black and one white square. If the covering were possible, then there would have to be equal numbers of black and white squares—but, since the two opposite (corner) squares removed have the same colour, this is clearly impossible.

(ii) Given any $n + 1$ integers from among the set $\{1, 2, 3, \ldots, 2n\}$, there must be at least two among them that are mutually prime, i.e. that have HCF equal to 1.

Here two separate perceptions are needed; namely, that *two adjacent integers have HCF 1*, and that, among $n + 1$ integers between 1 and $2n$, there must be two that are adjacent.

Each of these well-known problems is uncommon in the sense that in each the solution derives from insight; in the one case from a helpful formulation or *model*, and in the other from identification of a significant feature: how is a pair of coprime integers most likely to occur in the given situation? (Note that in both problems insight might be derived from experimentation—but this is not always possible.)

The art of problem-solving takes us, as indicated above (page 1), by gradual stages into what is described as "classical algebra" in the book in this series entitled *Algebra*. As problems become harder, and as we strive increasingly for generality, the use of letters for numbers becomes standard, and the techniques for solving problems require independent study. The lessons of arithmetic must not be forgotten; for what we do again and again is to search in general situations for the patterns observed in the real number system. Thus it may be helpful to think of polynomials as generalizations of integers, so that factorization of polynomials puts us in mind of the fundamental theorem of arithmetic, the remainder theorem recalls the division algorithm, and the decomposition of rational functions into partial fractions builds on familiarity with the rational numbers. Just as real numbers describe the geometry of the straight line, so vector spaces may be introduced as arithmetics of points in higher dimensions, with structures imitating as closely as possible that of the real numbers. This is how the pioneers in the nineteenth century proceeded, and they were motivated less by the urge to generalize than by the wish to construct mathematical frameworks for physics. They found that in the plane the structure of ordinary arithmetic can be recovered almost completely, in the shape of complex numbers (only order had to be sacrificed); that in four dimensions we have to sacrifice also the commutative law of multiplication, but that we then obtain the quaternions, a number system well suited to quantum mechanics; and that in eight dimensions a further sacrifice, this time of the associative law of multiplication, leads to the so-called Cayley numbers. It was found that, apart from these few exceptions, vector spaces must, inevitably, have a much weaker arithmetical structure than the reals; nevertheless, the concept of a vector space remains profoundly important in physics, no less than in mathematics, precisely because the structure of a vector space rests in so many ways on ordinary arithmetic.

However, this is the beginning of another story. Let me conclude by reminding the reader that mathematics is about solving problems; that the urge to solve problems is as old as mankind itself; and that to transcend stupidity by force of reason is a basic instinct of human intelligence. How splendid it would be if people, when asked what they had got in school from mathematics, were to reply that they had learnt how to tackle problems!

1 Objectives

The title *Number* for a book concerned with work for pupils in the age range 11 to 16 may require some explanation. If the work covered is not just "arithmetic", then what exactly is it? To obtain an answer, it is useful to examine briefly some of the objectives of recent changes in mathematical curricula at school level. Thus:

> The work should be relevant and enjoyable and form a sound foundation for the mathematical-type thinking needed in this statistics-computer age. The presentation should use the strengths of modern language and notation, and in particular set notation, relations and mappings, operations and structure. The material should be presented so that the discovery aspect of learning receives due emphasis.*

An attempt to draw up a list of *objectives* for any activity directed towards this broad aim is soon seen to be a very *subjective* operation, and any such list requires background explanation. For our "Objectives in Number" we list the following five:

N1. Basic numeracy: numbers in relation to one another.
N2. An understanding of the use of measures and approximations: numbers in relation to measurement.
N3. An understanding of the number-line: numbers in relation to geometry.
N4. An understanding of the real number system and its main subsystems: numbers in relation to algebra (and analysis).
N5. An appreciation of elementary number theory: pleasure in number.

We shall consider these in turn in some detail, but we stress from the beginning that they are not independent.

N1. Basic Numeracy

What, ideally, should each adult member of a modern society know about numbers and be able to do with them; and, in particular, what should the relevant training in this work be like for various pupils in the age range 11 to 16? It is virtually impossible to draw up a list of essentials which everyone would accept without leaving out important matters by accident (or prejudice!), or including things which are fashionable in some quarters but would be considered undesirable in others. We therefore put forward the following list of basic needs in numeracy, not as definitive, but as a stimulus to the reader to compile his own:

(i) Familiarity with the natural numbers (positive integers $\geqslant 1$), especially up to 100, their decimal representation, and their order. The operations of addition, subtraction, multiplication and simple division. A good knowledge of multiplication facts up to 10×10.

(ii) Familiarity with simple fractions as operators* and with their rational number notation.

(iii) Meaning of 0 (zero) and negative integers. (These will be needed, for instance, for temperature readings.)

(iv) Rational numbers in decimal form with place value, their addition and subtraction, integral and fractional multiples. (These are particularly relevant for calculations with money and metric measurements.)

(v) Percentages and ratios and the corresponding fractions, e.g. for percentage wage and price increases.

(vi) Social arithmetic, including pricing, wages and salaries, taxes of all kinds, interest rates (compound and simple), hire purchase, profit and loss, depreciation rates, mortgages, subsidies, pensions, sickness and unemployment benefits, social welfare of various kinds, household budgets, balance of payments, inflation, exchange rates, local, national and

---

* *Some Aspects of Syllabus Development, Evaluation and Revision, illustrated by the work of the SMG* (Scottish Mathematics Group), J. Hunter, 1972.

* Fractions as operators are discussed further in chapter 3, p. 36.

international trade and expenditure, imports and exports, and so on.

(vii) Elementary numerical combinatorics, probability and statistics to cope with the growing use of numerical facts and statistics in advertising, in guiding public attitudes to smoking, drinking, exercise, etc., in using sampling for polls and other types of market research, in describing the use of simple pictorial or tabular distributions and in giving a meaning to words such as average, mean, likely life-length, etc.

The teaching and learning of this work begins, of course, in the primary school and continues into the secondary school. Able pupils can cope with all of it at a relatively early age, while the less able will take much longer to absorb these ideas; their mathematical programme should be solidly based upon these basic needs.

N2. An Understanding of the Use of Measures and Approximations

We are confronted every day with the need to make or to understand numerical measurements in a wide variety of contexts: the height of a door, the weight of a letter, the length and width of a piece of dress material, the area of a lawn, the volume of a tank; speed limits, rates of petrol consumption in miles per gallon (or litres per 100 km), tyre pressures, electrode gaps; the noise level of *Concorde* in decibels, the frequency of a transmitter in megahertz, the temperature of a deep-freeze in degrees Fahrenheit or Celsius; population growth rates, the average length of life of an electric light-bulb, the half-life of radioactive waste...; some very simple and known to everybody, some very sophisticated and understood only by a few, yet all alike expressed in numbers. In every case of a number obtained by practical measurement, it is important to realize that it is approximate, that it is subject to possible errors of measurement, and that it may have to be held within certain tolerance limits.

In some ways this traditional part of arithmetic has been simplified; the introduction of decimal currency has removed the need for handling awkward units such as shillings and pence, and the process of metrication is removing the need to learn the imperial units such as ounces, pounds, stones and tons; pints and gallons; inches, feet, yards, miles, and the corresponding square and cubic measures. It is true that this process is taking place rather slowly, because of the capital invested in hardware geared to the old system, and also that favourite measures like the dozen will continue to be used for a long time, but already there is a considerable saving in teaching time, and the psychological battle to "think metric" is being won in the primary schools.

Problems of mensuration and the use of rates, etc., require facility in multiplication and division of decimal numbers; it is useful for pupils to have available various numerical aids such as tables, ready-reckoners, slide rules, desk calculators, pocket electronic calculators, and to acquire skill in the use of them.

The fundamental idea in any physical measurement, exemplified perhaps most clearly by standard techniques for finding a mass on a chemical balance, or by the use of "go/no-go" gauges, is that of repeated bracketing of the measure by numbers above and below, to an increasing degree of precision. In theory this process can be continued until any desired degree of accuracy is achieved; in practice this is never the case, and there comes a time when any further precision is impossible, or indeed ludicrous—as it is, for example, to give the distance between towns to the nearest metre, or the mass of a large sack to the nearest gram. A realization of this is important, as is the corresponding way of recording measurements "to the nearest..." or to so many significant figures. The length of a room can, for example, be measured (with care) to the nearest centimetre; it will then be given, say, as 4·27 m, and this means—and should be understood to mean—that it is between 4·265 and 4·275 m. In the same way, to give a mass as 2·730 kg means that it is known to lie between 2·7295 and 2·7305 kg, whereas a mass of 2·73 kg is merely known to lie between 2·725 and 2·735 kg. This usage should be adhered to, although children do not at first find it easy to understand.

There is a link here with the placing of irrational and other real numbers on the number-line which we shall discuss in the next section. In learning about $\sqrt{20}$ we make statements like "$4·45 < \sqrt{20} < 4·55$", and it is a surprising fact that, although we can increase the precision of such statements indefinitely (given sufficient patience and computing power!), we can never make an exact statement of this kind.

N3. An Understanding of the Number-Line

Throughout the age-range 11–16, the pupil is accumulating experience of numbers in different contexts through the medium of concrete examples. Some of these we have been considering in the last section. Numbers may be used to count populations, to measure lengths, to indicate masses, prices, rainfall, and so on. It is natural to represent these numbers as *points* on a scale, and to plot them as bar charts, or in graphical form. The ubiquitous ruler provides us with a ready-made model for locating points in this way.

We soon find the need to move from this static concept of a number to the dynamic idea of "numbers in motion" to represent changes up or down, paying in or drawing out money, speeds to left or right, and so on. In this way is born the idea of a number as a *shift*; the time has come to introduce *directed numbers*. These too can be related to the geometric display of scale movements and corresponding shifts on the number-line. Perhaps also in geometry we need at this stage to measure rotations clockwise or anticlockwise; and when we come to draw the graph of $\sin \theta°$ (for example) we need to "unwrap" the scale of $\theta°$ from the circle, where it naturally belongs, to the number-line.

As soon as we discuss scale drawing, proportion, and so on, the idea of enlargement arises, and we need numbers for scale-factors. The slide projector is an instrument for enlargement, as is a microscope or a pair of binoculars, and the scale-factor may well be engraved on the instrument in the form "$\times 6$". More interestingly, the camera is an apparatus used (usually) for "ensmallment" or reduction, and the problem of successive reduction or enlargement is a natural one, and leads to an explanation of a statement like $\frac{1}{3} \times \frac{1}{4} = \frac{1}{12}$. To be even more precise, both the camera and the enlarger have *negative* scale-factors, so that we have an approach to the problem of attaching a meaning to $^-2 \times {}^-3$. Ultimately we relate all this again to the representation on the number-line, which acts throughout as a sort of compendium of information on number, and should be permanently on display.

So far we are close to the spirit of the Greeks of the age of Pythagoras who recognized as numbers only the ratios which they could construct geometrically; like them, our pupils will probably as yet have no concept of any other sort of number. Indeed, it may be doubted whether some of them ever will. This is the subject-matter of our next objective, as at this point it is worth showing that compasses enable us to put a number like $\sqrt{2}$ on the number-line, and this should be done—preferably practically—as soon as Pythagoras' theorem is discussed. It is easy to show, using compasses and squared paper (but ensure that the scales each way on the squared paper are the same!), that $1·4 < \sqrt{2} < 1·5$. Closer approximations can be found with large radii and great care, but the staggering fact that $\sqrt{2}$, constructed in this way, will always fall *between* the points of subdivision is unlikely to gain immediate acceptance. The legendary fate of the unfortunate Pythagorean who discovered it will be of interest (see Introduction, page 3), even though the proof given by Pythagoras may be beyond the reach of many pupils.

In this way we can build up a geometrical representation of numbers which suggests their fundamental properties; at a later stage, probably in the sixth form, we may want to study these properties in a more systematic and abstract way. The time is then ripe for the reverse process—the arithmetization of geometry—and the proving of geometrical properties by appeal to algebra.

N4. An Understanding of the Real Number System and its Main Subsystems

While N3 is an objective of practical value which most pupils should be able to attain, N4 raises subtleties which may well be beyond the scope of many. A fuller discussion is given in chapter 9, and a much more thorough treatment than can be given in this book is to be found in David Wheeler's monograph *R is for Real*, published by the Open University. Here we content ourselves with a few suggestions for opening up windows.

A4 paper has its length and width (approximately, of course!) in the ratio $\sqrt{2}:1$. Chop off the largest possible square from a sheet; what is left is a narrow rectangle with sides in the ratio $1:\sqrt{2}-1$

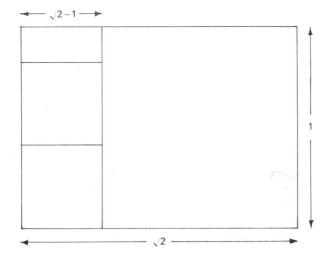

$= \sqrt{2}+1:1$. Chop off two squares from this and you get an even smaller rectangle *of exactly the same shape*. This process can then be repeated, getting successively smaller rectangles with sides in the ratio $\sqrt{2}+1:1$. Each side of the rectangle is less than half the size of its predecessor. If $\sqrt{2}$ were rational, we could construct the first rectangle with its sides both a whole number of units, say $m \times n$. Then the next similar rectangle would measure $(m-2n) \times n$, again two whole numbers, with $(m-2n)$ less than $\frac{1}{2}n$, and so

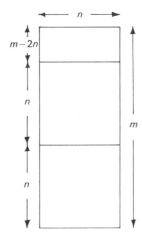

on. But we cannot go on halving a whole number without ultimately reaching a number less than one. A rectangle whose sides are integers which are less than 1 is an obvious absurdity. Therefore $\sqrt{2}$ cannot be rational.

π will probably be approached first by experiment—almost as a piece of physics. The simplest way is to wind a thread several times round a cylindrical can and then to measure it, thus finding the circumference; the diameter of the can can be found with calipers, and an approximation to π can then be computed. Archimedes *proved* (with great labour) that $3\frac{10}{71} < \pi < 3\frac{1}{7}$, but the most that pupils in this age-range can be expected to understand is the proof from perimeters of inscribed and circumscribed hexagons, that

$$3 < \pi < 2\sqrt{3}.$$

Sooner or later pupils discover that, while some fractions give decimal expansions that terminate, most do not. $\frac{1}{3}$ produces $0\cdot333\ldots$ with the same digit going on for ever—itself a surprising discovery. But there are obviously other decimals, like π, that neither terminate nor recur, and these must belong to numbers too—must, though it should be admitted there is some difficulty in grasping what those numbers are, or how to handle them. In some such way the problems associated with the real number system begin to appear; at this stage it is probably best to establish the intuitive idea that any real number has a decimal expansion, and that any decimal expansion corresponds to a real number, and to leave it at that.

As to the subsystems—the natural numbers, integers, rational numbers—a fuller and more systematic treatment is given in chapter 9. Opinions differ about the value of formal treatment of these systems, but it is our view that understanding comes through experience before the need for formalization is felt. In the words of George Polya: "Logic is the lady at the exit of the supermarket who tots up the value of the contents of the baskets which she has not collected". It is the job of the teacher of the 11–16 age range to see that the pupils collect the contents of the baskets. Much of the logical evaluation can safely be left to the sixth form.

N5. An Appreciation of Elementary Number Theory

Number theory used to be regarded as of interest to a few able pupils only. Certain algorithms, such as finding HCFs and LCMs, were taught more widely, but only with a view to enabling pupils to manipulate fractions. For our purposes we can define number theory as the investigation of properties of the integers, notably those which arise from the interrelation of their additive and multiplicative structures.

At an elementary level we should consider two aspects of number theory:

(a) Certain results in the theory are used, often unconsciously, in calculations: for example, the uniqueness of prime factorization, and simple ideas of congruence, such as the fact that all multiples of 5 end in 0 or 5, and no square can end in a 7.

(b) Some investigations into the properties of the natural numbers require only the simplest calculations, and are well within the capacities of our pupils, yet may lead children rapidly to striking results which could be difficult, or (in the present stage of our knowledge) impossible, to prove.

As an example of the first aspect, consider the finding of the factors of 253. There are several underlying results which make the work easier. Usually they arise as pieces of advice from the experienced teacher:

(i) Obviously neither 2 nor 5 is a factor.
(ii) There is a simple test for 3 as a factor, and it is not satisfied.
(iii) We need try prime factors only, so the next are 7, 11, ...
(iv) If 253 has factors, one must be less than 16 (since $16 \times 16 = 256$).

Each piece of advice is based upon the knowledge of some result in number theory, and so an additional reason for including such results might be to improve calculating facility. We give a selection of examples of the second aspect in chapter 10. In suggesting some investigations into numbers at an elementary level, we have in mind also that this could be a first stage towards the understanding of proof.

Elementary number theory can be described roughly as the body of basic results for N, the set of natural numbers, that depend on the division identity $a = qb + r$ by which an integer a on division by a positive integer b produces a quotient q and a remainder r satisfying $0 \leqslant r < b$. When $r = 0$, the positive integer b is called a *divisor* or *factor* of *a*, and *a* is called a *multiple* of *b*. The work includes number bases, least common multiples, greatest common divisors and the Euclidean algorithm for determining these, prime numbers, unique factorization (the fundamental theorem of arithmetic), simple congruences and arithmetic modulo *m*, numbers with special properties, some simple Diophantine equations such as $x^2 + y^2 = z^2$. From this list it is clear that many ideas from elementary number theory are spread throughout the whole range of school work on number, but a strong case can be made that at present this work is inadequate and undervalued. Much of it is suitable for discovery and project activity; it can bring teaching and learning in the subject close to a "laboratory-type" situation in which exploration takes place that might lead to conjectured statements and the idea of trying to prove results.

Many unsolved problems in elementary number theory can be easily stated and understood at a relatively early age and this helps, probably more than in any other subject, to emphasize that mathematics is still a live activity. In addition, at almost all levels within this subject, we can find large numbers of problems that can interest, stimulate and give pleasure to many pupils, and such work should strengthen their confidence in dealing with numbers.

Having dealt with our five objectives for "Number" in some detail, it may be helpful to end the chapter by reminding ourselves of the list:

N1. Basic numeracy: numbers in relation to one another.
N2. An understanding of the use of measures and approximations: numbers in relation to measurement.
N3. An understanding of the number-line: numbers in relation to geometry.
N4. An understanding of the real number system and its main subsystems: numbers in relation to algebra (and analysis).
N5. An appreciation of elementary number theory: pleasure in number.

2 Review of Books

2.0. Introduction

It is an interesting exercise to look at the development of the teaching of arithmetic during the present century. The evidence of early textbooks indicates a strong emphasis on practice in numerical techniques, in the use of a variety of different measures, and on practical applications, chiefly in the fields of commercial transactions and of mensuration. This emphasis has steadily declined, for a number of reasons. Repetitive exercises were felt to breed boredom and dislike of the subject; many imperial measures have become obsolete, and more will follow; the advent of various aids to calculation has seemed to make it less necessary to train clerks capable of faultless mechanical manipulation of figures. Simultaneously there has been a tendency to bring the investigation (though not, of course, the proofs) of some of the more interesting results in the theory of numbers into earlier years of the school curriculum; for example, the use of different scales of notation, which was formerly treated with thoroughness as a piece of sixth-form algebra, is now used for illustrative purposes in the primary school.

In the 1960s came the so-called "modern mathematics" whose far-reaching effects are with us today. While some of the more extreme forms of this, which have been in vogue in some other countries, have been avoided in Britain, there has been considerable change of emphasis in many parts of school mathematics. The most sweeping changes have been in geometry and algebra, but arithmetic has not been unaffected.

The innovators of those days felt, probably rightly, that there was much "dead wood" in the traditional arithmetic course; undoubtedly they expected metrication and standardization of units to proceed more rapidly than has in fact been the case. They also felt that a greater emphasis on the structure of number-systems and the place-value system of representation of numbers would bring greater understanding and thus lead to more accurate computational work. Their increased attention to number patterns and investigations was intended to provide greater interest in what had often been a dull routine. The good teacher has always contrived to interest his pupils; the claim that more teachers have been encouraged to do so can perhaps be substantiated. Regrettably, however, there is little evidence that computational skill has improved correspondingly.

The algorithms of computation, evolved by the human mind over the centuries, are easy only to those who are thoroughly familiar with them. They are not all that easy to explain, and it may well be that our later objectives N4 and N5, however desirable we may consider them to be on educational grounds, may be found difficult to attain even by the most skilful teachers using the most imaginative methods. There is no "royal road" to any kind of mathematics.

Our purpose in this chapter is twofold. We propose to examine books which span the last 70 years, seeing how the approach to number has developed during that period, and we propose to compare three major projects of the 1960s which have now become well established. Throughout our review, we shall keep in mind the objectives listed in chapter 1. We consider the following texts:

Arithmetic, G. W. Palmer, published by Macmillan & Co. Ltd. (1907)

The Teaching of Arithmetic, F. F. Potter, published by Sir Isaac Pitman & Son Ltd. (1936)

School Mathematics Project, Books *A–H* and *X, Y, Z*, published by CUP (1968–74)

Modern Mathematics for Schools (second edition), Scottish Mathematics Group, published by Blackie/Chambers (1971–75)

Midlands Mathematical Experiment, published by Harrap (1967–71)

2.1. *Arithmetic* (*chiefly examples*) **by G. W. Palmer**

As suggested by the title, this book omits general explanations and uses worked examples to describe methods. In the few places where algebraic discussions appear, it is stressed that these may be too difficult and can be replaced by special cases.

The first twelve chapters are the following:

the four rules; compound quantities; decimals (1); metric system; factors and multiples; fractions; brackets; averages; ratio; proportion; variation; decimals (2).

Applications of arithmetic are strongly represented in the later part of the book as follows:

percentages (profit and loss); square root; area of rectangular surfaces; volume of rectangular solids; mensuration of other figures; practice; approximation (absolute and relative error, significant figures, rough approximation, limits of accuracy, etc.); logarithms; interest and discount; shares and stock.

The last two chapters on "questions solved graphically" and "miscellaneous problems" suggest how more able pupils were occupied when they had completed the other topics.

Interesting features of this book are that "Factors and Multiples" and "Brackets" merit chapters in their own right, and that mensuration and approximation should receive so much attention. In fact the chapter on "Factors and Multiples" occupies only five pages, the last of which consists of a list of the usual digit tests for divisibility by 2, 4, 8, 5, 3, 9 and 11, with the introductory statement: "The following tests should be explained to the pupil".

The chapter itself begins with the statement: "For the meaning of factor, prime factor, etc., see the Glossary".

Chapter VII on "Brackets" occupies $5\frac{1}{2}$ pages and, although it does not mention words like associative, distributive and commutative, it contains useful numerical illustrations of the use of brackets.

In chapter VI on fractions, the only justification for $\frac{7}{12} \times \frac{5}{6}$ $= \frac{7 \times 5}{12 \times 6}$ appears in an exercise, and is preceded by the phrase: "Assuming that $\frac{7}{12} \times \frac{5}{6}$ means the same as $\frac{5}{6}$ of $\frac{7}{12}$". The justification is the reasonable one:

$$\frac{1}{6} \times \frac{7}{12} = \frac{1}{6} \times \frac{6 \times 7}{6 \times 12} = \frac{7}{6 \times 12}$$

Thus

$$\frac{5}{6} \times \frac{7}{12} = 5 \times \left| \frac{1}{6} \times \frac{7}{12} \right| = \frac{5 \times 7}{6 \times 12} \left(= \frac{7 \times 5}{12 \times 6} \right)$$

Division of one fraction by another is defined to be multiplication of the first by the *reciprocal* of the second. Essentially no recognition is made of a fraction as an "operator".

The book is not a "cookbook" in the sense that it does not give great lists of problems of identical type. It places enormous responsibility on any teacher using it, since he will have to supply all motivation, explanations and proof, where appropriate. It is in marked contrast with many recent texts which sometimes appear to tell the teacher how to think.

So far as the five objectives of chapter 1 are concerned, this text deals only with N1: Basic Numeracy, and N2: Measures and Approximations.

2.2. *The Teaching of Arithmetic* **by F. F. Potter**

This book is a text for colleges of education and for teachers rather than for pupils. It is in many senses a rich and remarkable piece of work that expresses a point of view roughly halfway between that of 1907 and that of the present day. The objectives N1 and N2 for number are adequately represented, but objective N3 which involves the pictorial power of the real number-line is essentially not mentioned. Objectives N4 and N5 begin to be considered, since the algebraic structure of the set of real numbers is developed to some extent, and the value of number theoretic ideas is strongly supported.

So far as structure is concerned, words such as *commutative* and *distributive* appear for the first time. Under the heading "Formal Multiplication", the author makes the following statement:

It is in multiplication that we first meet the fundamental laws of arithmetic in actual use. These laws are usually termed—(*a*) the commutative law, (*b*) the distributive law.

The *Commutative Law*. This states that additions and multiplications can be performed in any order, i.e.

$$x+y = y+x, \quad \text{and} \quad x \times y = y \times x.$$

It is interesting that these are combined in *one* law.

The *Distributive Law*. In symbols:

$$a(b+c+d+ \ldots) = ab+ac+ad+ \ldots$$

Factor Law. To these two laws is sometimes added a third, the Factor Law, which states that multiplication can be performed either with the whole number or by consecutive multiplications with its factors.

This law of course implies, in particular, that

$$(x \times y) \times z = x \times (y \times z)$$

i.e. that the *associative law* for multiplication holds, but this is not mentioned in the book, nor is the associative law of addition. Although identity elements, inverses and abstract structure do not appear in the book, this is hardly surprising when we remember that in 1936 many universities in Britain did not teach courses in abstract algebra.

Number theoretic ideas appear in several places in the book. For example, the following activity is suggested for early arithmetical work:

From any given whole number which is a square the next consecutive square can always be formed by simple addition. The following example will show the method:

$$(12)^2 + 12 + 13 = 169 = (13)^2$$
$$(13)^2 + 13 + 14 = 196 = (14)^2$$
$$(14)^2 + 14 + 15 = 225 = (15)^2$$

Similarly $\quad (30)^2 + 30 + 31 = 961 = (31)^2$

Two other examples mentioned for early investigation are:
(1) $1+3+5+ \ldots +(2n-1) = n^2$ (given, of course, for $n = 1, 2, 3, \ldots$, and illustrated geometrically), and
(2) magic squares.

However, the author's attitude to the use of number theory in teaching number is openly expressed in the following section:

Problems in the Theory of Number. To the mathematician the Theory of Number has always proved a most fascinating field of study. Its problems are infinitely varied; many have been solved with difficulty; many are still unsolved, though most remarkable discoveries have been made in the properties of numbers. Much of this work is of course entirely out of place with young scholars and students, yet when the difficult and unsuitable parts have been omitted, there is a remainder of an elementary yet most attractive nature, which will suggest interesting and profitable quests for (older) scholars. We suggest a few topics and problems which will be found useful.

Divisibility
(*a*) Complete the following numbers according to directions:
235* so as to be divisible by 9
456* so as to be divisible by 6
2*75 so as to be divisible by 15 (three solutions).
(*b*) Why must the product of any three consecutive numbers be divisible by 6?
What will be the corresponding divisor for four consecutive numbers?
(*c*) Why must the difference of any two numbers composed of the same figures in opposite orders be divisible by 9?

Squares. These provide endless problems of interest:

   (1) What is the smallest number by which 56 may be multiplied so that the result is a perfect square?

   (2) Any *odd* number may be expressed as the difference of two "neighbouring" squares, thus $13 = 7^2 - 6^2$, $19 = 10^2 - 9^2$, $37 = 19^2 - 18^2$. Why is this?

The author goes on to say that such problems should not form part of class exercises but could brighten up the dull round of class work and cause the pupils perhaps to reflect upon the "eeriness" of number. He adds that mathematical seed thus sown by the enthusiastic teacher may bear fruit of untold worth.

It is refreshing to find in a book written in 1936 such a clear and strongly worded support for such work.

         *   *   *   *   *

Sections 2.3, 2.4, 2.5 which follow, contain reviews of the Number work in three important British projects on modern school mathematics. The reviews are based upon reports by three experienced serving teachers. Although they demonstrate the fact that different teachers look for different things and points of emphasis, the statements cast light upon some of the contrasts between these three major projects. Each of these courses provides a sound treatment of arithmetic, and we hope that these reviews will help teachers in selecting material from them.

2.3. *SMP Books A–H* and *X–Z*

SMP is one of the older, and the most widely used of the "modern" courses, and the books reviewed here represent the later version of their course. *Books A* to *H* were originally designed for "non-GCE" streams, and *Books X* to *Z* are designed to extend *A* to *G* to an "O" Level course. Typically we would now expect to find *A* to *H* used as a CSE course, with *A* to *G* plus *X* to *Z* as the "O" Level

course. In some schools *A* to *G* plus either *H* or *X* to *Z* are used across the ability range, including sub-CSE pupils.

One of the aims of the pioneers of "modern" school mathematics was the elimination of drill routines of dubious value, and some users of *SMP* would feel that it has, if anything, gone too far in this direction, especially in the realm of Number. Many of the exercises go so far in the direction of eliminating boring repetition in favour of varied questions that they eliminate the beneficial near-repetition which builds the confidence of pupils, especially those of average and below average ability. Consider a particular example, Ex. D in chapter 4 of *Book C*, question 1:

(a) 0.02×0.03;	(b) 0.02×0.003;	(c) 0.006×0.02;
(d) 1.02×0.7;	(e) 7.5×0.02;	(f) 1.2×0.012;
(g) 40×0.02;	(h) 70×0.04;	(i) 600×0.09.

The purpose appears to be practice in the drill of multiplication, but the first seven questions all have different combinations of placing the decimal point in the two numbers to be multiplied. This would almost certainly be fine for pupils of above-average ability, but presents a speed of variation which the average or below-average pupil would be liable to find too much, and hence discouraging. The lack of drill routines has been recognized by *SMP* as they have published a document entitled *Manipulative skills in school mathematics* and also a series of booklets containing supplementary exercises.

Throughout the course, the aid to calculation that is mainly relied on is the slide rule, which is assumed at first to have C and D scales only. For this reason, in the treatment of trigonometry, the use of conventional trigonometric tables is introduced before the use of the corresponding scales of the slide rule (*Book F*, chapter 7 vis-a-vis *Book G*, chapter 6). Again, since sufficient accuracy is expected from a slide rule in straightforward multiplication and division, the chapter in *Book X* on "Using Tables" deals in some detail with squares, square roots and reciprocals, but completely ignores logarithms, which do not appear until *Book Y*. *SMP* were working from a situation in which they felt that logarithms were overvalued and slide rules were ignored. Perhaps they have gone too far in reversing this situation.

One of the sources of some concern among both users and critics of *SMP* arises from the assumptions made about the level of experience and the skills of pupils beginning the course at the age of 11. In the area of number, the assumption seems to be that little can be expected to be known about either vulgar or decimal fractions, since both concepts are introduced (albeit fairly rapidly) from scratch; but a considerable familiarity is assumed with addition, subtraction and multiplication (including long multiplication) of the counting numbers, since these topics are never treated specifically, and some facility with them is assumed in chapters 1 and 4 of *Book A*. The *SMP* authors have claimed that their motive in dealing with number bases early in the course (*Book A* chapter 4) is to revise the techniques used in base 10 by indirect means. There is room for scepticism both as to whether the knowledge is transferable in the way they hope, and whether pupils have enough confidence in the techniques concerned for this type of indirect revision to be adequate. Even chapter 1 of *Book A* assumes a familiarity with multiplicative number-bonds ("tables") which many teachers find does not tally with their experience of average and below-average pupils.

The organization of number work throughout the course is interesting, with some concentration of the work in the early books, but not as much as would be the case in a more "traditional" course. For example, to defer the subject of multiplication and division of decimals until nearly the middle of *Book C* (after Christmas of the second year), and the idea of a recurring decimal until early in *Book F* (middle of the third year) is an extreme position which lets down many science teachers, while being quite justifiable in terms of how they fit into the overall pattern of the course. On the other hand, the slide rule is also introduced (at least in principle) in *Book C* (beginning of the 2nd

year), which is quite early by more traditional standards. It is a pity that this introduction of the principle is not followed up with detailed practice until *Book E* (early third year). The timings above assume a rate of progress of two books per year, which is what was designed by the authors; more time can be spent on the later books if five years are available to CSE, but it is not wise to take too long over *Books A* to *D*. The faster pace must be maintained to complete the "O" Level course.

We now look at the *SMP* course in the light of the objectives N1 to N5 of chapter 1.

N1. BASIC NUMERACY

The probably over-optimistic expectations in the area of simple counting-number arithmetic, and the unsuitability of many of the practice exercises for the average and below-average pupils have been noted above. It could also be doubted whether the course gives pupils enough practice to maintain the skills they have acquired early on. In our experience, this approach is well judged for pupils of above-average ability, but needs a very considerable amount of supplementing for the average pupils in a comprehensive school.

N2. MEASURES AND APPROXIMATIONS

Once again, rather optimistic assumptions are made about the knowledge and level of confidence of pupils beginning the course. The current edition is metric throughout, in a popular rather than a strict SI form (i.e. centimetres occur rather than millimetres). Imperial units are ignored, except where they are useful as illustrations of different number bases. In this respect *SMP*, in common with most mathematics courses and examinations, is perhaps a little too far ahead of everyday life for the best convenience of the pupils (we still buy both milk and beer by the pint, and we are likely to do so for some years yet; where are pints in this course?). The practical collection of numerical data, and considerations of approximation and tolerances are well integrated into many parts of the work.

N3. THE NUMBER-LINE

The concept of the number-line is present implicitly throughout, mainly in the use of graphs. It is made gradually more explicit as the course develops. The concept of the rationals being dense among the reals is not made explicit, nor clearly implied by anything in the course. This is probably a realistic omission for the age-group concerned.

N4. THE REAL NUMBER SYSTEM AND ITS MAIN SUBSYSTEMS

The relationship between these is not explicitly considered in the CSE course, but is treated briefly in *Book Y*. For some reason the authors here talk about *P* as the set of positive whole numbers rather than the more usual *N*, associated with the names "natural numbers" or "counting numbers". Why this departure from a generally accepted notation? A working knowledge of what can and cannot be done in each system (algebraic laws being illustrated and used without too much overlay of jargon) comes through clearly, even when not explicitly laid out.

N5. ELEMENTARY NUMBER THEORY: PLEASURE IN NUMBER

The course gives the student plenty of opportunities to find pleasure in number which can be further developed by the right kind of teaching, although not all fall within our definition of number theory (chapter 1, page 15). For many pupils the chapters on Pascal and Fibonacci and on Napier's Bones will provide the most fun with numbers.

A few general points have been left until last because they relate not only to SMP's treatment of Number, but cover its wider aspects. The books are attractively presented and give the pupil an excellent chance to explore some of the byways of the subject as well as the main highway. However, with pupils of average and less than average ability, there are very few chapters with which a pupil could be expected to make much progress without pretty intensive teacher support. This limitation derives from

(*a*) the diversity of the types of example in each exercise, mentioned above; and

(*b*) the relatively high reading-age required by some of the explanation (and some of the questions).

This has two consequences in practice. Firstly the course requires a teaching methodology based fairly heavily on class teaching rather than individualized techniques, and is therefore not really suitable for a full mixed-ability system of organization, even in the early years. (This criticism can probably be levelled at almost any course based on a series of books.) Secondly, the use of the books with pupils of reading age lower than their level of mathematical attainment would be very limited. In such groups, the book is probably of more use to the teacher than the class. *SMP* have, however, produced a set of work-cards for individualized learning, which cover the first two years' work and which have been well received.

The applications of mathematics are present in many chapters, but often only in passing. Some teachers will feel that more specific discussion of, for example, wages, taxes, interest, etc., is needed to supplement the course. Others will feel that this need should be met outside the mathematics department.

In addition to the specific work on number (listed at the end of this chapter), there are many chapters where the use and manipulation of numbers play an important part without being the central subject of discussion, most notably the chapters on Statistics (six chapters in all over *Books A* to *G* and *X*, and review chapters in *H* and *Z*).

Sets of transparencies which reproduce the diagrams in the books are available; several of these relate to the number-line, but of course a simple scale for projection can be devised easily by any teacher.

2.4. *Modern Mathematics for Schools* **(2nd edn.), Books 1–7, by the Scottish Mathematics Group**

The publication of this series of books began in the middle 1960s, and a second edition, very thoroughly re-written, is now complete. There are nine books altogether in the series: the first seven cover the ground for the Ordinary Grade of the Scottish Certificate of Education examinations in mathematics (and in Arithmetic, which is a separate "O" Grade subject in Scotland) and would be suitable for virtually any GCE "O" Level syllabus. The course is started at age 12 in Scotland, which is the age of transfer. The books are fairly extensively used in England, and widely in other countries. Each book consists of separate sections on Algebra, Geometry and Arithmetic (and, in the later ones, on Computer Studies, Calculus and Trigonometry). While this approach might encourage some teachers to adopt a non-unified presentation, it can, and should, be a source of strength as it allows the teacher freedom of choice as to the order in which topics are presented: pupils are used, of necessity, to "jumping about the book" from one topic to another. The compartments are also by no means watertight: much of the most crucial work on number is to be found under Algebra rather than Arithmetic. For example, negative integers are met in chapter 3 of the Algebra of *Book 2* and the headings "An extension of the number-line", "The set of integers", "Order", "Addition on Z", "Additive inverse", "Subtraction", and "Review of sets of numbers N, W, Z, Q" suggest that the approach is very algebraic. The apparent necessity to include a section on Arithmetic in each of seven books means that such a vital (and essentially simple) topic as elementary estimation of error—absolute error, relative error, tolerance—is postponed until *Book 7*. We comment on this again later.

It is obvious, however, that the overall treatment of number has been carefully thought out, and progresses in an orderly way through the series. Much emphasis is laid on the different number systems; each book starts with a reminder of the accepted notation for the natural numbers, whole numbers, integers, rationals and real numbers (and primes). Much use is made of these in the text: in an exercise on solving simple equations, one question frequently asks "solve for x ($x \in N$)" and the next will demand solutions for the set of rationals, and so on, in order to give practice in understanding the differences between the number systems. There is an opportunity for the teacher to emphasize the necessity of enlarging the number system to accommodate the solutions.

Book 1 has a wide-ranging modern discussion on the system of whole numbers, i.e. the set $W = \{0, 1, 2, 3, \ldots\}$ with the usual operations and associated laws, and important subsets of W, and introduces the real number-line. One of the first pictorial uses of the real number-line and "vector addition" of numbers is the following:

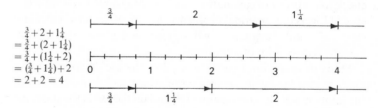

The operation of obtaining the LCM in order to add or subtract fractions is assumed known.

In *Book 2* the set Z of all integers is introduced as part of the Algebra, the heading of the first section being "An extension of the number-line". At this stage order on the number-line is also described.

In *Book 3*, Algebra, there is a long fairly algebraic chapter on the integers and rational numbers.

In *Book 4* the set R of real numbers is described, together with the real number-line, within the section on Algebra.

The foundations of number work, such as the four rules for

natural numbers, positive fractions and decimals, factorization and primes, is interspersed with the usual applications; there are chapters relating to money and measurement in *Books 1* and *2*, to statistics in *Books 2, 4* and *6*, to social arithmetic in *Books 3* and *6*, and to probability, time-distance-speed, the use of tables, the slide rule, mensuration, estimation of error and different counting bases more or less where we would expect to find them in the order of things. There is a feeling, however, that the whole Arithmetic section has been "stretched" to fit the seven books: the Statistics chapters in *Books 4* and *6* contain much overlapping material on histograms, etc., and on measures of central tendency. It is claimed by the authors that such revision has proved essential in practice.

The treatment of calculators and of aids to calculation now looks dated in the age of the cheap electronic calculator. Emphasis is—happily—laid on obtaining quick approximate answers as a check to accuracy of calculation, and on using algebra to aid some special forms of numerical problems; questions such as "calculate $999^2 - 1$", and "evaluate $\frac{1}{2}mv^2 - \frac{1}{2}mu^2$ when $m = 10$, $v = 74$, $u = 26$" receive a lot of attention.

Many examination boards now allow the use of calculators in mathematics (and arithmetic) examinations, and we expect that in the future much less emphasis will be laid on the use of the slide rule and logarithm tables as calculating devices. Until the textbooks catch up, everyone involved in the teaching of computational techniques is clearly going to have to do some basic thinking to reassess priorities and needs. This is discussed more fully in chapter 8.

Brief mention should also be made of the sections on Computer Studies, which occupy one chapter each of *Books 4–7*. The wide availability of computing facilities has clearly made some such series of chapters necessary in an integrated mathematics course. *Modern Mathematics for Schools* does its presentation through BASIC (after the initial necessary flow-diagram chapter in *Book 4*) which is as good a choice as any; some teachers using the books will feel the necessity to supplement these sections with their own notes in order to make the language match their own facilities.

Although the main emphasis is on computer programming, the first chapter on Computer Studies (*Book 4*) deals only with flow diagrams, and the third chapter (*Book 6*) is largely concerned with explaining how a computer functions. The endpoint of these chapters is the writing of programs to solve quadratics and do cosine rule calculations, which would be a challenge to more able pupils. There are opportunities to treat topics such as number sequences (*Book 5* Arithmetic) and the trapezium rule for area (*Book 7*) using algorithms, flow charts and possibly computer programs, but these opportunities are missed. Presumably the writers took the view that not all teachers will choose to include the computing chapters and the presentation adopted enables that choice to be made.

There is a variety of other publications connected with the Scottish Mathematics Group besides these seven books which are used by approximately the top 50% of the ability range. There is a series of *Mathsheets*—expendable illustrated worksheets designed for the less-able pupil—paralleling the exercises in *Books 1–3*. (The revised editions of the books contain many exercises labelled A and B, the B exercises being aimed at the quicker pupil.) There is a pack of overhead transparencies for *Book 1*, multiple-choice *Progress Papers* and answer keys for all the books, and, for pupils aiming at the arithmetic examination only, a single text, *Modern Arithmetic for Schools*, containing a summary of the arithmetic sections of *Books 1–4*, and the complete arithmetic sections of *Books 5, 6*, and *7*.

The summary gathers together the following topics: fractions; decimals; areas and volumes; ratio and proportion; social arithmetic (covering percentages, discount, simple interest, profit and loss); time, distance and speed; the slide rule; squares and square roots. However, it does not do full justice to the arithmetical content in *Books 1* to *3*, for it excludes the work on the number systems, described above.

Assessed against the five "Objectives in Number" this series of texts performs as follows:

N1. BASIC NUMERACY

On the whole well catered for. The chapters on social arithmetic in *Books 3* and *6* give a welcome emphasis to this aspect of N1, though they suffer from the inevitable defect that quoted rates of VAT, Income Tax, etc., are out of date. Statistics is thoroughly done, but with some repetition. Pupils are asked to calculate means, state modal classes, draw histograms and cumulative frequency curves, and estimate medians and inter-quartile ranges. They do not deal with variances, correlations, etc., and statistical distributions are regarded as histograms with no links to probability distributions. More could have been done to develop combinatorics and probability, particularly with a view to interesting the more-able pupil (this also has relevance in N5).

N2. MEASURES AND APPROXIMATIONS

This is adequately covered, although many teachers would like to see the estimation of error treated earlier and then referred to repeatedly in the continuing development. This type of question does occur, but late in *Book 7*.

> I am told that a rectangular room in a house measures 6 m by 9 m, both lengths being given to the nearest metre. What is (*a*) the maximum (*b*) the minimum area that the room might in fact have? If I am to carpet the room with carpet at £8 per m^2, what is the maximum outlay for which I should budget?"

This topic occurred earlier in the first edition of *MMS*, and was deferred to a later stage because it was found difficult by many teachers. Simple estimation of an approximate answer can be tackled early, but estimation of error size is undoubtedly more difficult.

The tables used are three-figure tables and the third significant figure is always treated as being true: this brings problems when one method using tables yields an answer 6·22 and another 6·23. Pupils deserve a reasoned answer at this stage (*Book 5*).

Teachers may not be familiar with the practice adopted to resolve the problem of rounding off, for example, 7·85 to 2 significant figures. The rule given is "when the preceding figure is even, round down, when odd round up; so 7·85 → 7·8 but 7·35 → 7·4". This has the effect of tending to balance out errors due to rounding off, and for this reason is often recommended in numerical computation.

N3. THE NUMBER-LINE

Extensive use is made of the number-line from as early a stage as possible. It occurs in discussions on inequalities, negative numbers, and the graphing of solution sets of equations, as well as its applications to the set of real numbers and the subsets thereof.

N4. THE REAL NUMBER SYSTEM AND ITS MAIN SUBSYSTEMS

The development $N \rightarrow W \rightarrow Z \rightarrow Q \rightarrow R$ is clearly seen to be essential to mathematical understanding, and is carefully done. (The logical basis formed can be useful later in an introduction to abstract algebra.) The extension $W \rightarrow Z$ for instance, is motivated by the necessity to solve equations such as $x+4 = 2$ as well as $x+2 = 4$, illustrated by examples from temperature scales and the like. It is a weakness of this approach that no simple method of convincing pupils that $(-6) \times (-3) = 18$ emerges; it is in fact made plausible by consideration of pattern in a table. Because this result cannot be "proved", many teachers may question the need for any attempt at a logical approach to the number system at this stage. Perhaps more could be done, at a later stage, to interest the able in some of the properties of the reals and the rationals—but this belongs more to the next section.

N5. ELEMENTARY NUMBER THEORY: PLEASURE IN NUMBER

Some interesting facts and conjectures are pointed out, but there is a feeling that an opportunity has been lost here, particularly with the introduction of B exercises in the second edition. Perhaps much of the fault lies in the fact that there are no real teachers' books—the teachers' editions contain a few differently-coloured pages per chapter in the present version, usually setting out the aims and objectives of the chapter. There would seem to be a real opportunity here to produce some material which, while it would be inappropriate in the text, would stimulate the teacher to excursions into elementary number theory—as has been said, many conjectures in this area are remarkably simple to propose (though not always so simple to solve). Why, for instance, should any intelligent pupil go through the course and yet be unaware of the simplicity and difficulty of Fermat's Last Theorem?

2.5. *Midlands Mathematical Experiment*

The *MME* course was initiated in the early 1960s by a group of working teachers using a syllabus devised by Cyril Hope. The set of books which we are considering was begun in 1967 and the last volume was published in 1971. There are five books, one for each year: *Volumes IA* and *IB* are for use in the 11–13 age range; *Volumes IIA, IIB* and *IIC* each have two versions, one leading to GCE standard and one to CSE. There is also *Excursions from Mathematics*. The *MME* was originally aimed at the above-average ability range, but there has since been some thought given to the rest of the ability range; e.g. Holland & Rees, *Maths Today, Books 1–4* (Harrap). In this review we shall consider only the GCE course.

In the first volume (i.e. *IA* and *IB*) red type is used to emphasize important points; it is a pity that the second volume was not printed in a similar way.

Most of the number work is done in the first volume: seven out of fifteen chapters in *IA* and ten out of fourteen chapters in *IB* are devoted to number or arithmetic. Only five of the thirteen chapters in *IIA*, two of the fourteen chapters in *IIB* and none in *IIC* are specifically on number work.

On the whole the chapters are long and contain a great deal of subject matter. For example, chapter 13 in *Volume IA* on Decimals starts with place value; converts fractions to decimals and vice versa; explains addition and subtraction of decimals using money and other metric quantities as examples; it deals with multiplication and division of decimals by integers and decimal numbers; it discusses recurring decimals and gives a few problems using metric quantities. The chapter continues with work on decimal places and scale reading with possible $\pm$ error in reading from scales; there is some practice in measuring lines and in writing numbers to different (given) numbers of decimal places. There is some work on conversion charts; half a page on the measurement of time, and of extremely small thicknesses using a micrometer screw. There are then two and a half pages on the iterative method

of finding a square root using $a_{n+1} = \frac{1}{2}\left(a_n + \frac{N}{a_n}\right)$ until a_n and a_{n+1}

agree to the required number of decimal places. The chapter ends with an introduction to percentages (expressing percentages as fractions and vice versa), pie diagrams and bar graphs with some discussion work on random sampling. All this is in the space of twenty-four pages.

Mathematical language is introduced at a very early stage in the course; the associative law of addition and multiplication, and the distributive rule for the natural numbers are mentioned in the third chapter of the first book; the existence of identity elements for addition and multiplication, and the meaning of closure under a particular operation are also explained at this stage.

The text includes simple direct questions for which the student can get a "right answer"; questions which lead to exploration (measuring objects, finding out about "things", e.g. the mass of *Concorde* in metric tons); and questions leading to class discussion (for example questions on sampling). In general there is a shortage of examples for practice. There are enough for the ablest pupils, but the teacher needs to augment the examples to give sufficient practice for the less able. The text tends to be more theoretical than experimental.

We will now consider the five objectives as proposed in chapter 1.

N1. BASIC NUMERACY

Familiarity with the natural numbers and the ability to perform the four rules with them is assumed. In *Volume IA*, chapter 7, fractions are introduced by expressing shaded parts of a diagram as a fraction of the whole. The pupil then divides twelve 24 cm × 12 cm rectangles into $1, 2, 3, 4 \ldots 12$ parts, so that the equivalent fractions, e.g. $\frac{1}{3}, \frac{2}{6}, \frac{3}{9}$, can be recognized. Addition and subtraction of fractions are performed by using equivalent fractions, e.g.:

$$\tfrac{1}{3} + \tfrac{1}{2} = \tfrac{2}{2} \times \tfrac{1}{3} + \tfrac{3}{3} \times \tfrac{1}{2} = \tfrac{2}{6} + \tfrac{3}{6}$$
$$= \tfrac{5}{6}$$

and the following exercises range from simple problems such as $\frac{1}{2} + \frac{1}{2}$ to the more difficult $\dfrac{a}{bc} + \dfrac{b}{ac}$ in a matter of 93 examples! The chapter ends with some work on patterns of numbers and on some simple infinite series; e.g. $\frac{1}{2} + \frac{1}{4} + \frac{1}{8} + \ldots$.

Negative integers (as additive inverses of positive integers) are not used until as late as the middle of the second year. Percentages and ratios are adequately covered in the course.

The social-arithmetic content mentioned in N1(vi) (page 11) is not adequately covered. The numbers of questions on simple interest, profit and loss, and depreciation are very few, and most of the listed topics are not mentioned at all.

Elementary numerical combinatorics, probability and statistics are often considered. Probability is introduced through sampling predictions as early as the end of the chapter on fractions (*Volume IA*, chapter 7). The chapter on Competitions, Communications and Computations (*Volume IA*, chapter 8) covers simple combinations; for example, the number of possible meals from a menu having a choice of three main courses and two desserts. The probability chapter (*Volume IB*, chapter 16) provides plenty of examples for the student to experiment with (dice, cards, tops), and so to compare with theoretical probability. The questions have proved successful, though perhaps too boy-orientated.

N2. MEASURES AND APPROXIMATIONS

Various simple and historical calculators such as the abacus and Napier's bones are mentioned. In *Volume IA*, chapter 8, the work on the powers of 2 leads naturally to logarithms to base 2, and finally the construction of a simple handmade slide rule, in base 2, is described. In the second year there is a chapter on significant figures and estimations which leads into the work on simple logarithms to base 10 for numbers greater than one. The student is then shown how to make a simple slide rule using a logarithmic graph, and this leads to the use of the slide rule which is encouraged throughout the course and in the "O" Level examination papers towards which the course works. Negative characteristics are dealt with at the end of the year, so that by the end of the first two years the student is expected to be able to use readily both logarithms and slide rule. As we have previously stated, there is some work on approximations and errors in the first book and a little in the other books. Areas and volumes are dealt with extensively throughout the course.

N3. THE NUMBER-LINE

The number-line, as such, is not mentioned in the course, although the student is encouraged at various stages to place first the fractions and then irrational numbers such as $\sqrt{2}$ and π on a line as an ordered sequence. On the other hand we have already mentioned the strong emphasis on measuring and approximations, and this work draws attention to facts about real numbers without dealing explicitly with the real number-line. For example, pupils could hardly remain in any doubt that between any two decimals there is another one.

N4. THE REAL NUMBER SYSTEM AND ITS MAIN SUBSYSTEMS

This is very adequately covered throughout the course, and the student is encouraged to look at the "laws" governing the number subsystems. The work is begun in the second year with a chapter on Number Sets which deals quite exhaustively with the natural numbers, integers and fractions, explaining the commutative and associative laws, and the closure property. (MME uses Z, Z^+, J, F to denote the number systems instead of N, W, Z, Q respectively; however, for the sake of clarity, we shall continue to use the more usual notation.) Consideration of the neutral element and inverse elements for addition leads to an extension of the whole numbers to the integers, and that of inverse elements for multiplication leads to the set of positive fractions (including 0). The chapter finishes with the idea of the whole numbers being embedded in the integers (for $+, -$) or embedded in the positive fractions (including 0) (for $\times, \div$). This is very formal for the second year (see chapter 9).

In the third year the work is amplified. The chapter on the Set of Integers considers subtraction in Z using the cancellation rule:

$$
\begin{array}{ll}
(+5)-(-2) = +5+[(+2)+(-2)]-(-2) & (+2)+(-2)=0 \\
\qquad = 5+2+[(-2)-(-2)] & \text{association} \\
\qquad = 5+2+0 & \text{cancellation rule} \\
\qquad = 5+2 & \text{neutral element} \\
\qquad = 7 & \text{addition in } Z
\end{array}
$$

Multiplication in Z is explained by two different methods. This chapter ends with some optional work on "Odd Arithmetic". The reader is given an operation $a \oplus b$ defined as $a+2b$ (i.e. $a+b+b$) so that $1 \oplus 1 = 3$ and $1 \oplus 3 = 7$, etc. From this the student is required to consider the associative, commutative and distributive

rules within this system, and the work is extended to $\otimes$ as repeated $\oplus$. This work can prove very interesting and thought-provoking to the brighter pupils, reinforcing the laws of ordinary addition and multiplication which they tend to take for granted. The chapter on the set of positive fractions is rather short, dealing with division as the inverse of multiplication and the distributive rule in the set.

Throughout the course there are whole chapters and parts of chapters dealing with sequences of numbers and limits. There is a small amount of work on iterative methods in the last book.

N5. ELEMENTARY NUMBER THEORY: PLEASURE IN NUMBER

The course deals quite exhaustively with number bases and modular arithmetic. The chapter on Modular Arithmetic in the first book looks at tests of divisibility for the numbers 9, 3, 5, 11, 4 and 8. In the fourth year the work looks at groups and isomorphic operations, and the chapter ends with an optional topic on Cyclic Subgroups.

There are only a few investigations in number theory.

2.6. The Number Content of the Three Reviewed Modern Courses

We list below the main headings of the number topics abstracted in chapter sequence from the modern courses reviewed. The headings are separated into five sections representing those topics that are intended to be covered during one year of the secondary school. In the case of MMS the timing given is the one used in Scotland; outside Scotland many schools begin with *Books 1–2* in Year 1, and so on, spreading the seven books over the five secondary years; the allocation of topics to years in the table would therefore need to be modified.

	SMP	MMS	MME
YEAR 1	Number patterns Number bases Further number patterns Division as repeated subtraction and as sharing Decimals Metric length and area Comparison of fractions Binary and duodecimal bases Directed numbers (the number-line)		Number bases Fractions Elementary permutations and combinations Powers and roots Modular arithmetic Decimals Area (rectangle, triangle, parallelogram, trapezium) Pythagoras
YEAR 2	Directed numbers (addition and subtraction) Multiplication and division of decimals Slide rule Multiplication and division of fractions Multiplication and division of directed numbers Punctuation and order Ratio Percentages Number patterns (Pascal, Fibonacci) Statistics (bar charts, mean, median, mode)	System of whole numbers, $(W = \{0, 1, 2, 3, \ldots\})$ (algebraic structure) Decimal systems of money, length, etc. Fractions, ratios, percentages Extension of number-line; Z and Q Decimals, metric system Computers (binary arithmetic) Statistics (bar charts, etc.)	Probability, distribution Significant figures, estimation Logarithms (simple cases) Slide rule Nomograms Ratio Number sets (N, Z and Q^+) Logarithms (more advanced) Volume of solids, density
YEAR 3	Square roots Pythagoras Slide rule Patterns with decimals (recurring decimals) The circle ($\pi \simeq 3$) Probability (introduction) Statistics (grouped frequency tables)	Algebraic structure of Z, Q Social arithmetic (accounts, banking, etc.) Ratio and proportion Probability (introduction) Time, distance, speed Set R of real numbers Squares, square roots Pythagoras (in the Geometry) Using a slide rule The circle (π, etc.) Statistics 2 (up to mean, mode, median) Computer studies (flow charts)	The set of integers Percentages Positive fractions (structure, etc.)

	SMP	MMS	MME
YEAR 4	Calculating (Napier's bones, etc.) Slide rule The circle (π) Percentages Computation (significance, approximation) Using tables Statistics (cumulative frequency, quartiles)	Logarithms Areas and volumes (prisms, cylinders, spheres, etc.) Number patterns and sequences Computer studies 2 (programs, BASIC) Social arithmetic 2 (money; expenditure of various types) Statistics 3 (up to quartiles, range and semi-interquartile range) Computer studies 3 (computers and their use in society)	Sequences, series and limits Introduction to Q Irrational and transcendental numbers (brief mention using $\sqrt{2}$ and π)
YEAR 5	Sets of numbers (N, Z, Q, R) Ratio, proportion and application of slide rule Units and dimensions Growth and logarithm functions	Irrational numbers (surds) Estimation of error (approximations, tolerance, etc.) Number bases Computer studies 4 (more programs in BASIC)	

2.7. Summary

Each of these projects provides scope for an interesting and exciting course in arithmetic, but in trying to evaluate them a teacher will want to ask many other questions about the treatment of other branches of mathematics, the level of writing, as well as practical problems of cost, etc.

The differences in arithmetical content between these projects are fairly small. *SMP* has probably the most radical ordering of topics, and places its emphasis in computation upon the slide rule.

MME has a lot of computation in the first two years, with not much emphasis upon number after this. *MMS* is perhaps a little more traditional and more practical than the other two, and places a greater emphasis upon different number systems.

Any of these courses offers exciting ideas as well as routine practice in basic numeracy. It is up to the teacher to ensure that both are covered by making an intelligent selection for his own pupils, augmenting his main choice of text, where necessary, by material from other sources.

3 Appreciation of Number

3.0. Introduction

It goes without saying that one of the aims of the teacher of mathematics is, and has always been, to develop in his pupils a familiarity with numbers and a facility in handling them, such as lies within their reach. We have already suggested that this is not an easy task, and that it calls for a high degree of skill, sympathy and devotion on the part of every teacher of the subject. It is doubtful whether there has been at any time, and certain that there is not at present, evidence which would justify complacency in this matter. Circumstances may change, but the fundamental need for numeracy, i.e. for confidence, understanding, and facility in handling numbers, remains the same. Columns of figures that forty years ago would have been tabulated and summed laboriously by hand can now be quickly printed and totalled by electronic devices; but the dissemination of cheap electronic calculators opens the door not only to more widespread facility in computation, but also to more widespread misunderstanding and misuse of figures uncritically transcribed.

Skill grows by practice; an understanding of the underlying theory may help the more intelligent pupil to master the rules, but the ultimate aim must be that the simpler processes can be carried out accurately without conscious thought. Undue emphasis on logical explanation may even confuse the weaker pupil. At the same time there should be sufficient understanding that, when the ground rules are changed (as, for example, when imperial units are replaced by metric, or percentages of cost price are replaced by percentages of retail prices), the algorithmic procedures can be modified without mental rejection.

In the sections which follow, we attempt to analyse some of the major components which go to make up a proper appreciation of number, and to suggest ways in which they can be acquired "without tears".

3.1. The Representation of Numbers

In order to operate successfully with numbers, a pupil clearly needs a sound understanding of the way in which symbols are used to represent numbers in the so-called Hindu-Arabic system. In short, the pupil must have a well-developed appreciation of "place-value" if subsequent number activities are to have meaning and interest for him. Materials which can be used to support the development of a child's concept of place-value include abaci of various types, Dienes' apparatus in base 10, and items such as matchsticks and straws which can easily be made into bundles of tens, hundreds, etc. We would expect to find all of these among the resources of a mathematics department in a typical secondary school today. (The question of multibase arithmetic is deferred until chapter 5.) This is not to say that *every* pupil who enters the secondary school will need to work with concrete representations of numbers, but there will be *some* whose number development is likely to be seriously hindered unless such materials are readily available.

Pupils need to reach awareness that the notion of place-value is a powerful aid to computation. The following simple example illustrates this idea, and the imaginative teacher will be able to produce similar items which start from a simple known fact and ask the pupil to deduce related results:

A pupil may *know* a number fact, i.e. he can recall that

$$6 + 7 = 13.$$

Does he realize that there are many related facts which he need not attempt to memorize? A few are listed:

$$36 + 7 = 43 \qquad 60 + 70 = 130$$

$$216 + 7 = 223 \qquad 0·6 + 0·7 = 1·3$$

etc.

A knowledge of the special role of ten and its powers is an integral part of the pupil's understanding of place value. A pupil who has difficulty in computing, say, $39 + 10$ or $436 + 100$ is clearly signalling that his understanding of place value requires attention. He needs more experience of the way the number system works; the teacher needs to diagnose the source of his difficulties and to provide appropriate remedial treatment, which will usually involve both careful explanation and a course of guided investigations or exercises.

3.2. Number Knowledge

What number facts should a pupil know so well that he can recall them almost instantaneously? While there is no absolute answer to this question, we suggest here some possible specific guidelines for the teacher.

As a first step, the teacher in the lower secondary school might ask himself whether he is devoting sufficient lesson time, energy and imagination to the teaching of addition and multiplication facts for single digit numbers. It seems quite clear that the boy or girl who does not know the table facts up to $10 + 10$ and 10×10 is at a serious disadvantage in the secondary school—or, indeed, anywhere. So there is a need for the teacher to provide *frequent* and *varied* bursts of number activity which have as one of their main goals the improvement of table knowledge. Such activity can take many forms, from the chanting of tables in unison to the classroom investigation which involves small whole numbers. Here are brief details of two activities which can be presented as games.

Cards labelled 1, 2, 3, 4, 5, 6, 7, 8, 9 are laid face upwards on the table. The two players select a card in turn and the winner is the player who first collects a hand containing three cards which total 15.

This is a game for two or more players which requires three dice, some counters and a number grid

0	1	2	3	4	5	6	7
8	9	10	11	12	13	14	15
16	17	18	19	20	21	22	23
24	25	26	27	28	29	30	31
32	33	34	35	36	37	38	39

A player throws the dice and uses the three numbers to make a number on the grid by addition, subtraction, etc., or some combination of operations. Thus a throw of 3, 4, 5 may be recorded by placing a counter on 23 since

$$23 = (4 \times 5) + 3.$$

Players score a point for each counter placed. In addition extra points may be scored for adjacent counters. For example, a player placing a counter on 26

would score 9 points ($1 + 8$ for the adjacent counters already in position).

As part of their knowledge of single-digit number facts, pupils need to be aware of the behaviour of 0 and 1 in combination with other numbers (so the table chanters should start at "no twos are nothing"!). Additionally, they should see the number system working for them in the sense that a knowledge of some multiplication facts for 2 is also a knowledge of corresponding facts for 20, 200, etc.

Teaching strategies for this particular aspect of number appreciation call for a high level of professional skill on the part of the teacher. Not only is there the need to provide a rich variety of arithmetical experience for pupils, but the teacher must be particularly alert to the attitudes of individual pupils in a context notorious for the threatening aspect it appears to have and the chips it provides for shoulders. For example, the weaker pupil particularly requires careful and persistent encouragement, but this must not reach the point where over-emphasis on the importance of knowing one's tables produces a strong antagonistic reaction in the pupil.

In learning multiplication facts, it is important that the pupil should realize that each "table" requires him to memorize the first ten numbers in an infinite arithmetical progression; i.e. that the steps in a *multiplication* table proceed by *addition*. There are useful observations to be made and questions to be asked about associated patterns. Some tables go even, even, even..., others go odd, even, odd... ; are there tables which go odd, odd, odd...?

To summarize this section, we consider that a high priority should be given to the learning of table facts up to $10 + 10$ and 10×10; that this should be carried out in a sympathetic manner by the teacher; that variety of style and method are important to avoid boredom and frustration; that the awareness of related knowledge should be regarded as an intrinsic part of "knowing your tables".

3.3. Whole-Number Operations—the Four Rules

In any first-year secondary class today, facility at addition, subtraction, multiplication and division is likely to vary considerably from pupil to pupil; so is the understanding of the operations themselves and the methods in use. This is not a new phenomenon, although the degree of variation in pupils' background has probably become increasingly marked as more primary schools have developed their own individual styles and philosophies in the provision of mathematical activity.

The chief responsibility of the secondary-school teacher in the current situation seems to be twofold: to establish and maintain friendly and effective working links with feeder primary schools, and to ensure that his starting points for incoming first-year children are appropriate to the pupils' previous experience. One hopes that the view that "mathematics only really begins in the secondary school" is nowadays completely discredited.

What are reasonable *minimal* computational goals which the teacher might wish most pupils to reach in the first year or so of a secondary school? Here is a list for discussion:

1. Addition (up to about five numbers) and subtraction, both involving numbers with no more than three digits.
2. Multiplication and division of numbers up to three digits by single digit numbers.
3. Some understanding of the procedures used which goes beyond an ability merely to set out the calculations "correctly".
4. A good understanding of the properties of, and the relationships between, the four operations.
5. A willingness and ability to estimate answers and to check them, where appropriate, by carrying out a related calculation.

In passing, we observe that the list attempts to take account of the availability of various calculating aids and devices. The following comments are intended to amplify the thinking behind each item.

1. In any class there are likely to be in use at least two methods of subtraction (more if variations in notation are included). This matter is taken up in chapter 5.

2. The teacher may decide to include multiplication by factors, where this is possible, in order to deal with two-digit numbers; for example 48×18 can be handled as $48 \times (3 \times 6) = (48 \times 3) \times 6$. However, while this has value for mental arithmetic, little time is saved in the long run for calculations to be done on paper; sooner or later long multiplication must be learnt. This is even more true

of division. Division by factors leads to endless trouble with remainders; long division is merely an extension of repeated subtraction, and has value in learning to understand the process, as well as in acquiring facility in computation. The use of factors should probably be confined to the removal of obvious common factors, as in simplifying fractions; e.g. $145 \div 25 = (29 \times 5) \div (5 \times 5) = 29 \div 5$.

Decisions about when and how to move from such statements as "$11 \div 4 = 2$ remainder 3" to "$11 \div 4 = 2\frac{3}{4}$" or "$11 \div 4 = 2 \cdot 75$" will also need careful thought and planning. The appropriateness of each of these answers depends on the context, and is discussed further in section 3.5.

3. Some pupils may not be able to understand the usual formal setting out of calculations if it is done without any explanatory material. It is worth while spending time in the early stages over writing out calculations more fully. For example,

(a) It may be helpful to go back to the full statement

$$\begin{array}{rcl} 20 \times 8 = 8 \times 2 \times 10 = 160 \\ 9 \times 8 = & 72 \\ \hline 29 \times 8 & 232 \\ \hline \end{array}$$

before using the abbreviated form

$$\begin{array}{r} 29 \times \\ 8 \\ \hline 232 \\ \hline \end{array}$$

(b) At the next stage, to multiply 29 by 18, we can write

$$\begin{array}{ll} 29 \times 10 = 290 & \text{side work} \quad 29 \times \\ 29 \times \ 8 = 232 & \qquad\qquad\quad 8 \\ \hline 29 \times 18 = 522 & \qquad\qquad\ 232 \\ \end{array}$$

before writing

$$\begin{array}{r} 29 \times \\ 18 \\ \hline 290 \\ 232 \\ \hline 522 \\ \hline \end{array}$$

(n.b. " $\times$ " is here read as "multiplied by", not as "times"; the order can be reversed for those who read it the other way).

(c) In an addition sum, the setting out

$$\begin{array}{ll} 73 + & \text{can precede} \quad 73 + \\ 29 + & \qquad\qquad\quad 29 \\ 42 & \qquad\qquad\quad 42 \\ \hline 14 + & \qquad\qquad\ 144 \\ 130 & \qquad\qquad\quad 1 \\ \hline 144 \\ \hline \end{array}$$

4. The observant teacher will realize that in (a) above the associative, commutative, and distributive laws for multiplication have all been used. There is no point in insisting on the technical terms, but children should be aware of these properties from their numerical experiences and know how to use them in multiplication and addition, even if they cannot express them. The common error in long multiplication of transposing the tens and units figures, e.g.

$$\begin{array}{r} 29 \times \\ 18 \\ \hline 2320 \\ 29 \\ \hline 2349 \\ \hline \end{array}$$

shows a lack of appreciation of what is going on when using the "rule of thumb" method they have been taught.

There is a school of thought which advocates that the whole operation should be written out in fully expanded form: thus

$$\begin{aligned} 29 \times 18 &= (2 \times 10 + 9) \times (1 \times 10 + 8) \\ &= 2 \times 10^2 + 9 \times 10 + 16 \times 10 + 72 \\ &= 2 \times 10^2 + 9 \times 10 + 1 \times 10^2 + 6 \times 10 + 7 \times 10 + 2 \\ &= 3 \times 10^2 + 22 \times 10 + 2 \\ &= 3 \times 10^2 + 2 \times 10^2 + 2 \times 10 + 2 \\ &= 5 \times 10^2 + 2 \times 10 + 2 = 522. \end{aligned}$$

This is a salutary exercise if it convinces the teacher that

(a) the standard algorithm for long multiplication is by no means a simple procedure;

(*b*) the use of place-value notation conveys enormous simplifying power;
(*c*) a child has a great many things to think about when doing a long multiplication sum.

Our own view is that it is clumsy and probably confusing to *write* all this out, but that certainly the concepts and processes involved should be made clear in *oral* teaching and by *practical* handling of materials.

> For example, the child needs to understand that 20 is twenty, which is two bundles of ten, so that 8×20 (eight twenties) is sixteen bundles of ten = 16 bundles of ten, which gives ten bundles of ten (a hundred bundle) and six bundles of ten, which is 60. Perhaps the best detailed breakdown of the process would be "18×29 is eighteen twenty-nines. This is ten twenty-nines and eight twenty-nines."

$$
\begin{array}{r}
29 \\
18 \\
\hline
\end{array}
$$

	200	"Ten twenties are two hundred;
	90	ten nines = nine tens = ninety
290	290	(ten twenty-nines so far).
	160	Eight twenties are one hundred and sixty (as above);
	72	eight nines are seventy-two
232	232	(that's the eight twenty-nines).
522		

Adding them all up gives 522 Hooray!"

Of course we do not expect all this to be present in the child's consciousness every time the algorithm is used; the object of the exercise is to get the pupil habituated so that all this comes automatically, and rapid and accurate computation is possible. But it is important that the full understanding can be recovered when necessary, so that the process can be modified for other needs, e.g. computation in other bases, or with decimal fractions, and not merely fossilized in the memory.

Perhaps this is the point at which to emphasize that teachers can learn much by considering why their pupils make certain mistakes; correcting computational work is not simply a matter of ticks and crosses. Ideally, exercises can be diagnostic as well as evaluatory,

and appropriate remedial treatment can be prescribed.

Pupils often tend to see the four rules as quite separate procedures; they should therefore be given plenty of opportunities to see the connections between them. Addition statements can be re-written in subtraction form, and vice versa, so that subtractions can (and should) be checked by addition. Multiplication and division are similarly related as inverse processes, though we now have the complication that division is not always exact. When it is, checking by multiplication is easy and should be encouraged; it is more difficult when there is a remainder, but the check reveals very clearly what is happening in this case. In this context it is important to consider multiplication as repeated addition, and division as repeated subtraction. Many of these procedures are effectively demonstrated on a mechanical desk-calculator, if such are still available.

The main goal throughout should be the acquisition of skill in computation, and of discrimination in applying it; knowledge which facilitates this, and encourages simplifying procedures (such as $19 \times 11 + 19 \times 89 = 19 \times (11 + 89) = 1900$) is to be welcomed.

5. Checking and estimation are no less important than the other skills. This is especially true if such aids to computation as slide rules, logarithms, hand calculators, ready-reckoners and electronic calculators are to be properly and effectively used. Pupil development in this depends on continual attention and reinforcement; the teacher therefore needs to be ready at all times to seize opportunities for asking for estimates before calculations are carried out, and for insisting that checks should be carried out, not by looking up the answer, but by the pupils' own activities. A child who knows before he starts operations that 18×29 is about $20 \times 30 = 600$ is less likely to be content with an answer of 2349.

In conclusion, we should perhaps reiterate that the matters we have discussed relate to the minimum computational skills to be aimed at in the first years of secondary education; it is to be expected that many children will have reached the majority of these goals before leaving primary school.

3.4. Fractional Numbers

So far our discussion of number appreciation has focused mainly on children working with whole numbers. Now we consider what experiences and understanding associated with fractional numbers contribute significantly to a child's basic appreciation of number.

It is generally asserted that more attention should be given to decimal fractions in view of the decimalization of our monetary system and the slow but steady change to a metric system in commerce and industry. This is obviously a reasonable view but, while accepting its force, we should not lose sight of the fact that a sound grasp of place value demands understanding of the *fractions* $\frac{1}{10}, \frac{1}{100}, \frac{1}{1000}\ldots$. Indeed, simple fractions are important in a variety of applications.

In working with fractions, it is important to develop children's awareness of several related viewpoints. We exemplify three of these by the following simple questions.

1. Ten children in a class of thirty are boys. What fraction are girls?

2. Express the red cuisenaire rod ⬜ as a fraction of the yellow ▭▭▭▭.

3. Three children share 2 sticks of rock equally. How much rock does each receive?

Question 1 is a "parts of a whole", or an "out of" situation. In question 2 the emphasis is on the comparison of two separate objects: we might call this the "ratio" view, and observe that the idea of inverse is implicit here:

red is $\frac{2}{5}$ of yellow
yellow is $2\frac{1}{2}$ times red

Question 3 is a "sharing" view of fractions, and reminds us that fractions are strongly associated with division of whole numbers.

Underlying all these aspects of fractions is the idea of a fraction as an *operator*. This can be brought out by amplifying the pupils' responses. Thus, in question 1, the response is "two-thirds". "Two-thirds *of what*?" "Two-thirds of the class". Similarly in question 2, "two-fifths *of the yellow rod*" brings out the dynamic relationship; and in question 3 "two-thirds of a stick" is the only possible answer. This aspect is probably closest to children's own experience; one breaks sticks into three, halves apples, divides pies into quarters, and so on. The very word "fraction" (="breaking") is derived from this idea.

It is when we come to multiplication that this aspect becomes all-important. Five half-slices of bread make two-and-a-half slices; five halfpennies make $2\frac{1}{2}$p; $5 \times \frac{1}{2}$ (five times a half) $= 2\frac{1}{2}$. These need only the static view of a half as something two of which make a whole. But it is different with $\frac{1}{2} \times 5$; what does it *mean*, anyway? If it is read as "a half times five", how can you take anything half a time? So we are forced back to the halving process: "Take half of five". "Double a piece of string five feet long back on itself and cut it in half". "Fold a strip of paper and halve it". "Make a scale-drawing of this half-size". A pantograph or a camera demonstrates this idea most effectively. A camera set to a fixed distance—preferably an old camera with a large ground-glass focusing screen—becomes a "tenthing machine", or, strictly, a "minus tenthing machine". It now becomes clear that the operation "take a half of" followed by the operation "take a third of" is equivalent to the single operation "take a sixth of", so that it is reasonable to say that $\frac{1}{2} \times \frac{1}{3} = \frac{1}{6}$. On the number-line, $\frac{1}{2}$ is the point we get when we halve the segment (01); $\frac{1}{3}$ is what we get when we third this segment; we get $\frac{1}{2} \times \frac{1}{3}$ when we do these two things in succession, halving $(0\frac{1}{3})$ or thirding $(0\frac{1}{2})$ to arrive at $\frac{1}{6}$ in each case. A mathematician would say there is an isomorphism between the composition of enlargements and the multiplication of fractions, but these distinctions need not be made explicit in secondary school.

It is natural to go on from this to the ideas of the neutral operator ($\times 1$) and the inverse of an operator—going back from the camera screen to the original object. This is one way of showing that $\div \frac{1}{2}$ and $\times 2$ are equivalent operations.

We claim that an appreciation of fractions should be based on the viewpoints outlined above, together with the concepts of equivalence (see chapter 9) and ordering. Given a list of fractions, can pupils identify those which are smaller than $\frac{1}{2}$, for example? Only when pupils have a satisfactory understanding of these ideas, which they can demonstrate by their ability to work with them, should they go on to formal methods of addition and subtraction. A final observation, which applies also to decimal fractions, is perhaps worth making. The number-line, showing whole numbers only, is a familiar sight in the primary classroom, but often little use is made of it at secondary level. The opportunity to fill in some of the points between whole numbers seems unfortunately often to be missed. This is a serious omission, both on practical grounds (the need to measure, read scales, etc.) and because the association of numbers with points on a line is a quite basic component of number appreciation.

The references to decimal fractions have been kept deliberately to a minimum in this section. We believe that the most important observations have already been made, at least in passing, in the earlier section on number representation, i.e. place value.

3.5. Application of Number

In the preceding sections of this chapter we have invited the reader to consider some aspects of a pupil's number development: place value, knowledge of tables, the four rules, etc. However, such a development will be seriously defective if the pupil has little or no opportunity to apply his growing range of knowledge and skills.

The message of this section can be expressed by the slogan "knowing *when* to multiply is as important as knowing *how* to multiply".

Our first set of questions concerns the meaning of division. Many pupils, even when they have decided that they have to divide, find it difficult to understand what they are doing, and what is to be done with the remainder, if any. Consideration of the similarities, and the differences, between examples of the following type may prove helpful:

1. How many cans costing 16p can be bought with a 50p coin?
2. A length of ribbon 50 m long is cut into 16 pieces of equal length. How long is each piece?
3. A speedboat travelling at 50 km/h passes a sailing dinghy travelling at 16 km/h; how many times as fast is the speedboat going?

There are really three separate ideas here; the first involves repeated subtraction, the second demands an understanding that $\frac{1}{16}$ of 50 m $= \frac{50}{16}$ m; the third involves equivalents for the rational number $\frac{50}{16}$. Answers such as (to 2) "3 m and 2 metres over", or (to 3) "3·125 km/h" reveal serious misunderstandings. This matter is discussed further in section 5.4.

The next selection of questions presents the pupil with a variety of simple situations in which he has first to decide on the appropriate computational step and then to carry it out—successfully we hope! Most texts produced during the last ten years or so have few examples of this type, and we encourage the teacher to recognize that simple problems such as this are a vital part of a pupil's early number development.

1. Brian has read 55 pages of his book. It has 124 pages altogether. How many pages has he left to read?
2. A tin of peaches costs 37p. The supermarket cashier rings up 73p by mistake. How much should she knock off the bill?

3. Find the missing dimensions (all in centimetres).

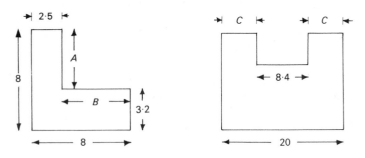

4. There are 120 children staying at school for dinner. If 8 children can sit at a table, how many tables will be needed?
5. A coach needs about 5 litres of petrol to travel 18 km. Estimate how much petrol it will use on a journey of 200 km.
6. Alan's grandfather was born in 1909. How old is he now?

3.6. Pupil Attitudes

We conclude the chapter with some observations on the factors which influence a pupil's attitude towards number. It seems reasonable to postulate that a boy or girl who has come to regard numbers as potentially useful and interesting will generally progress more easily and happily than the pupil for whom number is synonymous with boredom. Quite reasonably, pupils need to be persuaded that the amount of time and effort they are being asked to invest in number work will produce a meaningful return in terms of utility, interest and success.

If we accept this, it suggests strongly that the secondary-school teacher must provide for his pupils a rich environment of number. The diet must be a varied one: patterns, puzzles, games, investigations can help to provide a reasonable range of routine computational practice, but their exploitation needs to be carefully organized if they are to go beyond the mere provision of entertainment. Above all, they need to be put in a scheme which appears coherent *to the pupils as well as to the teacher*.

At all times the teacher must ask himself if he is building on success or reinforcing failure by trying to rush pupils through a particular stage of development so that they can do some "proper calculations which they should have learned to do at primary school anyway".

We hope that the general message of this chapter is clear. The development of an *appreciation* of the significance of number deserves to be given the highest possible priority at the secondary level, and should be regarded as the continuation of a process which started long before the child arrived in the infant school.

4 First Activities in Secondary School

4.0. Introduction

In this chapter we make some suggestions about number work for 11-year-olds—particularly for those who have just entered secondary school and so are faced with the problems sometimes associated with the transition from primary to secondary.

It is probably still true that most primary schools spend the majority of the time that is allocated to mathematical activity on number. Nevertheless different primary schools cover different selections of topics and spend varying amounts of time on consolidating the basic facts and skills. Close liaison between secondary schools and their main feeder primary schools is obviously advisable, where practicable, in the coordination both of content and of teaching methods.

Initial approaches in secondary schools vary considerably. At one extreme, tests on new entrants exhibit the inevitable weaknesses, and the first term is spent on revision, often with little light relief. At the other extreme, little effort is made to bridge the gap from primary to secondary, and a jump is made straight into new material without a check on the necessary prerequisites. For example, if pupils are unable confidently and quickly to give the answer to $23 + 10$ (in decimal notation), i.e. do not have a good understanding of place-value notation, then there seems little point in starting with the writing of numbers in different bases in order to try to consolidate the idea of place value (for a fuller discussion, see section 5.1). Other schools avoid number completely during the first term and then make an essentially new start in the second term.

Instead of following any one of the three possibilities just described, there are many ways in which transition activities in number can be introduced without giving the impression that the pupils are being tested, or that they are going over the same old ground again. These activities can help to improve the pupils' confidence in handling and using numbers, e.g. in recalling addition and multiplication facts, in understanding place-value notation, in developing confidence in using algorithms for arithmetical operations, in building up a useful vocabulary of number, and in generating a general awareness of numbers. The choice of a particular set of activities may well depend on the actual work that the pupils concerned did in their primary schools, and of course contacts between primary and secondary schools will help with this choice. The pupils themselves might well help by being asked to try to recall what they did on number in the primary school.

4.1. Statistics and Probability

In some cases, some sort of *statistical work* might make a suitable start, but it should be handled carefully, since often pupils have been drawing block graphs since they were five. For such pupils statistical work could be more than simple representation of data. A useful stimulus is to collect facts and figures from the whole population of the new first year, and this is best done by means of a duplicated questionnaire which they can fill in during their first mathematics lesson, asking questions about primary schools, family, pocket money, favourite this, that and the other, leisure activities, bedtimes, etc. If this activity is combined with practical measuring, then the pupils can also provide details about height, weight and other personal measurements, an important ingredient since subsequent analysis and representation will raise problems about continuous as opposed to discrete distributions. If there are enough questions, the questionnaire can be cut up into sections, and each section can be given to a small group of pupils who should produce appropriate graphs and summaries, perhaps with scattergrams where appropriate, e.g. to consider correlation between height and weight. More-able pupils might be asked the following type of question: Are taller children of the same age heavier? Are children who play a lot of games lighter? Do you lose weight if you play games? It is sometimes not possible to give definite answers to questions such as these, and we can point out that statistics is quite different from mathematics in this way. Such a project can be useful for getting to know a new intake quickly, as well as for making a subjective assessment of the pupils' abilities in using numbers.

Another statistical survey of this kind might be on TV programmes, where the data are available in the *Radio Times* and the *TV Times*. Data are easily gathered, and significant questions arise in the gathering process. What is a News programme? Which plays are being televised? When does evening viewing begin? As in the surveys of pupils, it is possible to use the data to ask further questions, e.g. Is more sport televised in summer than in winter?

Related to statistics there is the possibility of spending some time in the first year on *probability* as an aid to number confidence. Probability may be introduced through a variety of experiments, such as tossing coins, throwing dice, making and choosing cards, using a random-number table. The counting of different outcomes is a major part of such activity and, as in gathering information about the members of a class, data can be gathered inside the classroom.

Able children can begin to compare the "results of experiment" with the "expected results" in an informal way, since this comparison should be the main theme of work on probability in the 11–16 age range.

4.2. Number Games

"Number games" can also provide a useful and interesting experience during the transition stage. Since the possibilities are almost limitless, we cannot hope to provide a comprehensive list, and shall merely select a few to indicate some suitable ideas.

I. NUMBER SQUARES AND RECTANGLES. (ABILITY TO RECALL SIMPLE ADDITION AND MULTIPLICATION FACTS INVOLVING 0–10)

As an introduction let us ask ourselves how well we know and understand our tables. Here are some rectangles abstracted from a normal ten-by-ten multiplication square. Can you fill in the missing numbers easily, bearing in mind that there may be more than one answer in some cases? Who can find the largest number of different possible ways of filling in each square or rectangle?

But what about "knowing your tables"? As stated in chapter 3, the child of 12/13 who cannot recall addition and multiplication facts for 0, 1, .., 10 is at a serious disadvantage. His situation can be compared with that of a reader who has to struggle over each word; reading can hardly be a pleasure in such circumstances and, by analogy, a child is unlikely to derive much satisfaction in mathematics when simple computations cannot be disposed of quickly and confidently. This problem has already been discussed, but here we mention some number games that may help.

II. THE "THREES AND FIVES" GAME (using Cuisenaire rods)
This is a train of 3-rods and 5-rods

It is 19 units long.

What other lengths, up to 40 units, can you make with threes and fives? Try another pair of rods. What lengths can you make by putting different numbers of these end to end? (See chapter 10.)

III. MULTIPLICATION BINGO
Each pupil has a card with various products on it (see the diagram). The teacher or one of the pupils acts as caller, calling out various multiplication problems like 3×7, 4×12. The first pupil to cover his card wins.

3	18	14	15
27	25	36	24
63	35	56	50
21	72	33	81

IV. MULTIPLICATION MEMORY GAME
Here we have two sets of cards which are placed face down, one set on one side of a dividing line and the other on the other side.

One set of cards contains sums like $\boxed{3 \times 12}$ and the others numbers

that correspond to the answers $\boxed{36}$. Players play in pairs. The first player chooses one card from each set; if they match, he keeps them. If not, he replaces them and the next player tries, having seen the first player's draw and making use of that if appropriate. A successful go means another turn. The player with most pairs at the end of the game (or the end of the period) wins.

V. MULTIPLICATION SNAP
Here we have a pack of cards such that each card has a sum or an answer on it. The cards are then shared and played as in Snap. Note the importance of being able to read the cards both ways up!

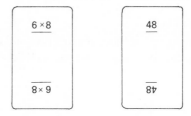

VI. MULTIPLICATION DOMINOES
A typical domino looks like this:

Each domino has a problem on its left-hand half and a number on the right. The usual domino rules apply, problems and answers being matched; there are no "doubles". Part of a game is shown below:

The game can be extended to include additions, subtractions, and divisions; a much larger stock of dominoes will then be required.

Various other number games exist, or can easily be devised, based on cross number puzzles, snakes and ladders, ludo, monopoly, use of dice, etc.

4.3. Applications of Number

The tables that record sporting results such as football league tables, cricket tables, or golf scores, are good sources of number activity. We illustrate this by two examples:

I. FOOTBALL TABLES

Eight teams make up the Smogsbridge Football League. Before last Saturday's game the league table was as follows:

	P	W	L	D	GF	GA	Pts
Athletic	4	4	0	0	12	1	8
Borough	4	2	0	2	6	2	6
Corinthians	4	3	1	0	7	3	6
Eagles	4	1	1	2	5	5	4
North End	4	2	2	0	5	6	4
Park Road	4	1	2	1	3	8	3
Tigers	4	0	3	1	2	7	1
United	4	0	4	0	1	9	0

The results on Saturday were:

Borough	4	Athletic	1
Corinthians	0	North End	2
United	3	Eagles	2
Park Road	3	Tigers	1

Rewrite the league table to bring it up to date, putting the teams in the correct order.

II. GOLF TOURNAMENT

Ten players took part, playing on a course with a par score of 72. The results at the end of 3 rounds were:

Name	Score	Name	Score
Smith	−9	Williams	0
Todd	−8	Neill	1
Robertson	−8	Taylor	1
Rankin	−4	Howard	4
Black	0	Brown	6

The scores are given relative to the par total of 216 for the three rounds. Now complete the final similar table for the four rounds of the tournament, given that the actual scores on the final round were:

Todd	67	Black	71
Robertson	69	Rankin	71
Smith	70	Taylor	72
Neill	70	Williams	74
Brown	70	Howard	74

III. DISTANCE CHART FROM THE AA HANDBOOK

1. You are based in Newcastle and plan to visit York, Leeds and Sheffield in that order. Find the total distance you must travel. Can you shorten the journey by visiting the places in a different order?
2. You are limited to travelling 160 miles a day. Give examples of the trips you could make from Manchester in a day if (i) you return to Manchester (ii) you don't return to Manchester.
3. By referring to a map and the chart, find the shortest journey from Northampton to Preston, visiting two other places on route.
4. Using the "given" map, on which Stoke, Sheffield and Lincoln are marked, and the mileage chart, mark the position of Nottingham as accurately as you can. (This will provoke some geometrical questions; why are the results not very good?)

Inverness
Aberdeen
Fort William
Perth
Glasgow
Edinburgh
Stranraer
Carlisle
Newcastle upon Tyne
Teesside
Kendal
Preston
Leeds
York
Hull
Liverpool
Manchester
Sheffield
Lincoln
Holyhead
Stoke on Trent
Nottingham
Norwich
Shrewsbury
Birmingham
Cambridge
Aberystwyth
Northampton
Hereford
Colchester
Carmarthen
Gloucester
Oxford
LONDON
Cardiff
Bristol
Guildford
Maidstone
Dover
Barnstaple
Salisbury
Brighton
Taunton
Southampton
Exeter
Dorchester
Penzance
Plymouth

Mileage Chart

Distances are given to the nearest mile and are measured along the shortest practicable route (not necessarily AA recommended) of classified roads.

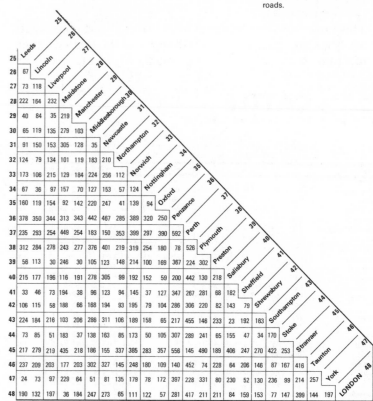

	Leeds	Lincoln	Liverpool	Maidstone	Manchester	Middlesborough	Newcastle	Northampton	Norwich	Nottingham	Oxford	Penzance	Perth	Plymouth	Preston	Salisbury	Sheffield	Shrewsbury	Southampton	Stoke	Stranraer	Taunton	York	LONDON
25 Leeds																								
26 Lincoln	67																							
27 Liverpool	73	118																						
28 Maidstone	222	164	232																					
29 Manchester	40	84	35	219																				
30 Middlesborough	65	119	135	279	103																			
31 Newcastle	91	150	153	305	128	35																		
32 Northampton	124	79	134	101	119	183	210																	
33 Norwich	173	106	215	129	184	224	256	112																
34 Nottingham	67	36	97	157	70	127	153	57	124															
35 Oxford	160	119	154	92	142	220	247	41	139	94														
36 Penzance	378	350	344	313	343	442	467	285	389	320	250													
37 Perth	235	293	254	449	254	183	150	353	399	297	390	592												
38 Plymouth	312	284	278	243	277	376	401	219	319	254	180	78	526											
39 Preston	56	113	30	246	30	105	123	148	214	100	169	367	224	302										
40 Salisbury	215	177	196	116	191	278	305	99	192	152	59	200	442	130	218									
41 Sheffield	33	46	73	194	38	96	123	94	145	37	127	347	267	281	68	182								
42 Shrewsbury	106	115	58	188	66	168	194	93	195	79	104	286	306	220	82	143	79							
43 Southampton	224	184	216	103	206	286	311	106	189	158	65	217	455	146	233	23	192	163						
44 Stoke	73	85	51	183	37	138	163	85	173	50	105	307	289	241	65	155	47	34	170					
45 Stranraer	217	279	219	435	218	186	155	337	385	283	357	556	145	490	189	406	247	270	422	253				
46 Taunton	237	209	203	177	203	302	327	145	248	180	109	140	452	74	228	64	206	146	87	167	416			
47 York	24	73	97	229	64	51	81	135	179	78	172	397	228	331	80	230	52	130	236	99	214	257		
48 LONDON	190	132	197	36	184	247	273	65	111	122	57	281	417	211	211	84	159	153	77	147	399	144	197	

5. Choose ten towns, list them according to position, starting from the most northerly town and working southwards. Keeping this order, construct a mileage chart for them. What do you notice about the figures in the rows and the columns?

IV. PRICE REPORT

This table lists the average market prices at certain markets for the five categories of fatstock cattle (*steers*: light, medium, heavy; *heifers*: light, medium) during a certain week and indicates the changes in these averages from those of the previous week,

+ denoting "dearer"
− denoting "cheaper"
= denoting "unchanged"
·· denoting "no comparison is possible".

The prices are given in pence per kg to the nearest 0·1 p.

Many questions or activities arise such as:
1. Produce the list of average prices for the previous week.
2. As a farmer, where would you like to sell your cattle?
3. As a butcher, where would you like to buy your cattle?
4. For how much would you expect to sell a 440 kg steer at Carlisle?
5. How much less might you expect to receive for an average priced 420 kg heifer sold at Hexham this week, compared with last?
6. It costs £30 more to send cattle to Ripon rather than to Tyneside; you may send up to 20 animals for this amount. How many 400 kg steers would you have to sell at the same time in order to make it more profitable to attend Ripon market?

CATTLE

Week's throughput 11,805+247

Market	Weight in kg	Steers Light 380–460	Steers Medium 465–555	Heavy over 560	Heifers Light 330–395	Heifers Medium 400–480	Total entry
Averages†		66·7−0·4	64·9−0·4	62·6−0·2	63·9−0·8	62·3−0·4	
North							
Acklington	(Th)	67·3+1·5	67·1+4·2	63·6+2·9	64·7−0·1	62·1+0·6	146
Belford	(Th)	69·7+1·7	68·4+3·9	68·6+5·3	65·7−2·5	68·2−0·1	134
Berwick	(F)	66·5−3·8	66·2−3·1	64·1−4·3	64·2−3·6	65·2−4·1	183
Bingley	(S)	..	..	..	64·7−1·3	..	103
Boroughbridge	(M)	68·2−2·2	66·0=	63·9=	67·9=	65·0−0·7	330
Carlisle	(M)	68·2−0·9	68·6+1·1	66·9+1·3	66·6−1·6	66·2+2·3	204
Darlington	(Th)	65·1+0·3	64·0+0·8	61·8+1·0	64·0−1·1	62·8+0·2	296
Doncaster	(Tu)	64·3+0·9	64·4+2·5	61·8+1·5	62·2−1·3	..	98
Driffield	(Th)	69·3+2·1	66·4−0·5	64·2−1·4	65·2−0·8	..	306
Gisburn	(Th)	67·7+1·3	66·5−1·5	..	65·8+1·4	65·5+3·2	55
Hellifield	(Th)	69·0+2·3	66·5+1·3	..	65·3+0·2	62·0−1·0	99
Hexham	(Tu)	63·9−3·6	62·8−4·1	58·6−6·6	61·1−6·4	60·8−5·7	65
Hull	(M)	..	66·2−1·1	64·5−0·2	..	65·5+0·8	120
Malton	(F)	68·1=	65·6+0·1	63·8−0·7	67·0−0·4	67·0+1·5	613
Morpeth	(M)	70·9+1·6	68·5+2·7	..	65·7−0·8	62·8−1·1	55
Otley	(M)	65·6−1·3	63·4−1·8	..	64·4−1·6	62·4−2·3	196
Pannal	(W)	65·1−3·1	64·4−1·9	..	61·7+2·5	60·9−2·1	185
Penrith	(M)	66·5−2·4	64·5−2·4	64·7−0·5	64·8−5·0	64·6−2·5	167
Preston	(Tu)	67·5−3·9	65·9−4·3	62·1 nc	65·2−1·7	63·4−2·5	486
Ripon	(W)	64·2−3·7	64·3−1·8	62·9−0·3	65·7−2·4	60·9−3·9	323
Thirsk	(Th)	68·0+0·5	66·5+1·6	64·0−0·4	64·6−0·6	66·5+1·7	391
Tyneside	(M)	..	64·9−5·8	..	64·8−4·7	63·8−6·8	89
Tyneside	(F)	62·6−1·7	62·0−1·0	59·7−1·1	62·4−0·3	62·0−1·8	204
Ulverston	(Th)	67·3+1·0	64·4−0·4	..	60·0+0·6	61·1−1·1	61
Wetherby	(M)	66·0−1·4	64·7−0·5	63·0−0·6	61·0−3·4	61·3−4·2	261
York	(M)	67·7+1·0	66·1+1·4	64·7+1·5	65·3+0·3	65·4−1·1	424

Reproduced by permission of *Farmers' Weekly*.

4.4. Number Investigations

The following investigations have been found successful at this level. Many other possible ones are given in chapter 10.

I. TAKE FOUR NUMBERS

```
    5    11      8     15
       6    3      7     10
         3    4    3       4
           1    1      1    1
             0      0        0    0
```

This pattern starts with the row 5 11 8 15. Numbers next to each other are subtracted (forming non-negative differences) to make the next row 6 3 7 10. Can you explain 10 at the end?

We get the 3rd row from the 2nd row, and so on.

Form the pattern which starts 19 7 4 26.

Choose other sets of four numbers and work out the complete patterns. Explanations need not arise at this stage.

II. RELATED OPERATIONS

As we mentioned earlier, addition, subtraction, multiplication and division are too often regarded by pupils as separate unconnected operations. There are many opportunities for helping pupils to think about various relationships between the operations. One simple question that illustrates the possibilities is the following:

$$17 \times 23 = 391.$$

Use this result to work out

$$18 \times 23$$
$$391 \div 17$$
$$17 \times 22$$
$$34 \times 23$$
$$17 \times 46$$

III. ONE TWO THREE FOUR

Copy and complete:

(a) $34 + 21$ =
(b) $(4 \times 3 \times 2) + 1$ =
(c) $4 - 3 + 2 - 1$ =
(d) $1 + (24 \div 3)$ =
(e) $3^2 + 14$ =
(f) $(4 \times 21) + 3$ =
(g) $4 \times (21 + 3)$ =

What other numbers (up to 100) can you make using the symbols $1, 2, 3, 4, +, -, \times, \div$ and any brackets required?

(All except 53, 56, 57, 74, 77, 89, 90, 94, 95, 97, 98, 99.)

The games, applications and investigations listed above illustrate an important activity that is part of the learning of mathematics at each stage, namely, that of building up mathematical vocabulary. At the first-year stage a number vocabulary might include words like odd, even, multiple, divisor, sum, product, difference, and so on, and problems can introduce and build up a knowledge of terms.

An example that illustrates this process is the following:

IV. A NUMBER CHAIN

This chain is formed by the rules:

(1) If a number is even, take half of it.
(2) If a number is odd, multiply by 3 and add 1.

The chain stops when the number 1 is reached.

Complete the chain given above.

Start with some other natural number less than 100 and complete the corresponding chain formed by the rules.

What is the longest chain you can find?

(An explanation in this case for what happens does not exist!) (See chapter 10.)

Other investigations can be used at the transition stage that introduce mathematical ideas that will be developed at later stages, such as some of those associated with *elementary number theory*. This approach might be typified by a lesson beginning as follows:

I have a sequence of natural numbers in mind that starts:
1, 2,
"What number comes next?"
3 is suggested, but rejected—baffled looks. Other suggestions are made, from which the teacher selects 4.
1, 2, 4,
"What next?"
Discussion. 8, because they double each time: 7, because the differences go up by 1 each time, and that determines the sequence that I had in mind,

1, 2, 4, 7,
Now the sequence can be continued. (How far?)

4.5. Other Possibilities

Other sequences can be started, alternative continuations can be discussed, and pupils can construct their own or lead the class. Sequences can also be developed from combinatorial situations in geometry, e.g. the triangular numbers arise from a consideration of intersections of straight lines. Work can include even numbers and other multiples, powers, Fibonacci numbers, squares, triangular numbers and primes. Some detailed suggestions for this type of work are given in chapter 10, sections 1 and 2. Out of all this can come work on divisors and multiples, fractions, decimals, series, indices, infinity, limits and logarithms. However, to begin with, the benefits are that pupils are free to discuss ideas about numbers, which is often a new experience for them, and that they become more familiar with numbers themselves, as distinct from merely operating with them.

Many other topics could be considered under the heading "First Activities in Secondary School" and some are discussed in detail in other chapters of this book. Multi-base arithmetic is mentioned in chapter 5, a history of arithmetical notation (which is also a fairly popular way of looking afresh at place value) is mentioned in the Introduction, the construction of simple calculating aids and the use of different calculating devices is included in chapters 6 and 8, and there are many other possibilities.

References

Number—some ideas for the classroom. Editor: David Hale. School of Education, University of Nottingham/Nottinghamshire Education Committee (March 1975).

Turning the Tables and *Numbers Everywhere.* Association of Teachers of Mathematics (East Midlands Region). Available from: ATM, Market Street Chambers, Nelson, Lancs.

5 Classroom Decisions

5.0. Introduction

Few would disagree with the proposition that the mathematics teacher today has to make many more decisions about the content and style of his work in the classroom than did those who taught him the subject. Not only has the whole educational climate undergone vast change in the last twenty years, but the particularly sensitive area of mathematics has been the object of widespread experiment both in syllabus content and in teaching methods whose success or failure is notoriously difficult to evaluate. This is a healthy development in so far as a wide variety of pupils are no longer forced into a single learning pattern (though it is doubtful to what extent they ever were), but it imposes on the head of department and even on the individual teacher much greater responsibility in the use of his greater freedom to choose mathematical themes and methods of working suited to his pupils' needs.

In this chapter we make three basic assumptions about the mathematics teacher:

(a) He will not be content to hand over his role as decision-maker to the textbook writer or to the committees that frame examination syllabuses.
(b) He will not wish to take decisions in isolation from his colleagues, and will therefore regard as crucial the process of group discussion within the school mathematics department by which decisions are reached.
(c) He will be equally concerned with the effect of activities in the mathematics department on the pupils' progress in other subjects, and will wish to include teachers of those subjects in the discussions which take place.

With these assumptions, the purpose of this chapter is to draw attention to the kind of question which must be asked, and the kind of criteria which must be applied for teachers to arrive at conclusions about the scope and emphasis of their work in arithmetic. This we shall do by taking specific examples of debatable areas where decisions may have to be made between alternatives which can each present a reasonable case for adoption. The following have been chosen for this purpose:

1. Multibase arithmetic.
2. Factors.
3. Standardizing computational methods.
4. The number-line.
5. Introducing directed numbers.
6. Introducing rational numbers.

The relation of arithmetic to science and other applications is discussed in the next chapter.

The first two areas have been influenced by recent curriculum development. If a textbook written during the last ten years is compared with any of its predecessors, it will almost certainly show an increase in the amount of number work in bases other than ten, and a reduction in the attention given to factorizing and associated ideas. The older book may contain no mention of the possibility of other number bases, and the newer one no reference to HCF or LCM.

The third area is one where the secondary-school teacher has always had problems in organizing first-year work with a varied intake from primary schools using widely different methods. Should he attempt to impose some sort of uniformity? Alternatively, can the very variety of pupils' experience be turned to useful advantage?

The last three areas are matters of vital concern, in which widely different approaches claim their supporters. They are also areas where inadequately prepared pupils can be left uncertain, confused, or completely bewildered by a new and unfamiliar approach.

This chapter does not pretend to answer the questions it raises, or to come to any prescriptive conclusions. Much will depend in every case on the knowledge and skill of the teacher, and the background and abilities of the pupils. But it does seek to pin-point the questions which need to be asked, and to provoke fruitful discussion. The mathematical background of much of the material in this chapter is treated more fully in chapter 9.

5.1. Multibase Arithmetic

(a) ARE THERE SOUND REASONS FOR INTRODUCING NUMBER BASES OTHER THAN TEN?

The reasons normally advanced are two: the value of the wider experience offered in understanding of place-value—on the principle of "What do they know of England who only England know?"—and the applicability in many fields in computing and communications of the binary (two-state) system. For example, the *SMP Teachers' Guide to Book A* states (p. 98):

> The purpose of this chapter is particularly to draw attention to the importance of position in our methods of writing numbers. It is not considered that the ability to count or calculate in bases other than ten is important in itself.

Is this a sufficiently strong rationale, and do the expected benefits follow? Can experiments with different bases help to illustrate conventional procedures in base ten?

Again (*SMP Teachers' Guide to Book B*, p. 220)

> This is the time to emphasize the idea of a "two-state system". With base two, it is either one state or the other, either yes or no, up or down, left or right, on or off, and it is this feature of the base which makes it so applicable to electrical circuits.

Is this a good reason for introducing the binary system? Are there facilities for exploiting the connection with logic and simple switching, if this is thought desirable? Will it contribute to the pupils' appreciation of the applicability of mathematics? To their general mathematical development?

How much work in other bases will need to be done before reinforcement and enrichment of ordinary number work can reasonably be expected to happen?

(b) GIVEN THAT WE DECIDE TO INTRODUCE OTHER BASES, HOW FAR DO WE GO? WHAT KINDS OF EXPERIENCE AND ACTIVITY ARE IMPORTANT?

Is it sensible to work initially in only one base other than ten and, if so, does it matter which one? Or should the pupils have early experience of several different bases (including at least one bigger than 10)?

What sort of priority should the teacher give to computation in bases other than ten? How valid is the claim that pupils will gain in confidence and understanding through adapting their methods for addition, subtraction, etc., in base ten to other bases?

At what stage, if ever, should pupils be given a standard procedure for conversion from one number base to another? What are the benefits of an *ad hoc* trial-and-error approach to conversion?

What materials are needed? Is a form of abacus sufficient, or should Dienes MAB (or something similar) be available to show more directly the representation of numbers in different bases?

(c) THE PUPIL'S VIEWPOINT

Is the pupil who has an insecure grasp of place value likely to be helped by a multibase approach? Or will the attempt to extend his ideas in this way, together with the associated problems of vocabulary and symbols, leave him even more confused? Are some ways of initiating multibase ideas better than others in the sense that they minimize the risk of confusion?

Certain results in arithmetic are dependent on the use of ten as the base of notation. Examples that come to mind are divisibility tests (a number is divisible by 3 or 9 according as the sum of its digits is so divisible); terminating and recurring decimals ($\frac{1}{5}$, $\frac{1}{4}$

terminate, but $\frac{1}{3}$ recurs with period 1 and $\frac{1}{7}$ recurs with period 6); the old party trick

> Write down any 3-digit number whose hundreds digit is greater than its units digit:

$$
\begin{array}{rr}
 & 745 \\
\text{reverse the digits} & 547 \\
\hline
\text{subtract} & 198 \\
\text{reverse the digits} & 891 \\
\hline
\text{add} & 1089 \\
\end{array}
$$

> The answer is always the same.

Will some pupils respond to the challenge of attempting to generalize such results by investigating what happens in other bases? The question of the period of recurring decimals can lead quickly into deep and difficult number theory.

Can some experience with other bases help a pupil to see, however dimly, that mathematics is a coherent whole, and that arithmetic and algebra are not disconnected topics? In particular, is it possible to link positional notation with the algebra of polynomials, by showing that

$$17 \times 23 = (t+7)(2t+3)$$

$$= 2t^2 + \text{seventeen } t + \text{twenty-one} \quad \text{in any base,}$$

and that what happens now depends on the base in use?

Is there a place for simple digit puzzles which give simple algebraic equations, such as the following?

> Find a two-digit number which is three times the sum of its digits.
> Explain why 121 is a square in any base.

5.2. Factors

(a) IN WHAT SPECIFIC WAYS IS A STUDY OF FACTORS LIKELY TO AID PUPILS' BASIC APPRECIATION OF NUMBER?

It was at one time thought that the use of factors enabled children to multiply and divide by numbers of two and three digits using the so-called "short" methods some time before they needed to learn the supposedly more difficult process of long multiplication and division. Is this argument valid today?

Does the use of factors help to undergird the knowledge of multiplication tables? Does it aid understanding of multiplication and division and their relation to one another?

Are divisibility tests worth teaching? Presumably recognition of even numbers and multiples of 5 can be expected—but what about multiples of 3 and 9? Can an adequate explanation be given at this stage? Does this help an understanding of number patterns, or linking arithmetic with algebra?

(b) HOW SHOULD FACTORS BE INTRODUCED?

Should we concentrate first on collecting multiples, by extension of multiplication tables, which leads on to one method of obtaining the LCM of two numbers? Or should we examine sets of divisors, e.g. set of divisors of $24 = \{1, 2, 3, 4, 6, 8, 12, 24\}$, which can lead on to discussion of perfect numbers and to a heuristic method of finding an HCF? Or should we begin by classifying numbers as prime or composite, and aim at prime factorization?

If we agree to define "rectangular" numbers, how do we do so? If the numbers are represented by arrays of dots, then a row of dots is not naturally thought of as a rectangle; but if by arrays of squares, a set of 5 squares in a row *does* form a rectangle and a pupil may wish to indicate $5 = 5 \times 1$ as a rectangular number. If so, *all* numbers are rectangular and the concept is pointless. The mathematician's word is *composite*, and "rectangular" is a pedagogical invention; the Greek word was *oblong*, which did not include the "squares". If we decide we need the term because of our interest in geometric patterns ("figurate" numbers), then it is best to use it in a distinctive sense, i.e. a number with two factors different from itself and unity.

How do we define a prime? If we agree on the definition of rectangular, then a prime is a number greater than 1 which cannot be drawn as a rectangle. The phrase "greater than 1" is inserted with the sole purpose of excluding 1 from the primes. Children (and their teachers) are often worried as to why 1 is not a prime; the plain fact is that we decide not to call it one, and we do this because we want to be able to say that any natural number has a unique factorization into prime factors. Several definitions have been formulated to make this appear more natural, such as

a prime is a number with not more than two divisors

but there is little point in such subtlety. It is better to say plainly

(*a*) 1 is not a prime.
(*b*) If a number has a divisor other than itself and 1, it is not a prime.

Primes are the numbers left after these others have been struck out (by the sieve of Eratosthenes).

(c) HOW FAR DO WE GO?

How much work should we do on HCF and LCM?
Are the set notation definitions likely to be helpful?

HCF of *a* and *b* = largest member of {divisors of *a*} ∩ {divisors of *b*}
LCM of *a* and *b* = smallest member of {multiples of *a*} ∩ {multiples of *b*}

Is it important to teach standard procedures for finding HCF and LCM? Will pupils benefit more if they devise their own?
How far can pupils get a feeling for such results as

If a prime *p* divides *ab* and does not divide *a*, then it divides *b*.

or

If *m* divides *a* and *b*, then it divides $a+b$ and $a-b$?

Presuming that no formal proofs are going to be given, should pupils get to the point where they know these facts to be true by accumulated experience? For example, should they see at once that 25 cannot be a divisor of 565, that 7 is a factor of 2121, and a statement such as $43 \times 53 = 29 \times 71$ is impossible? Where else in mathematics is knowledge of this kind likely to be useful?

(d) THE PUPIL'S VIEWPOINT

How will the slow learner respond to this area of work? Will he feel overwhelmed by new ideas, or attracted by the extra variety which appears in his number activities?

Are pupils likely to ask the purpose of the work? What is their likely reaction to a classroom approach which is investigational rather than one which is highly structured by the teacher?

How will the pupil see this work in relation to other parts of mathematics? How effective is it likely to be as a means of developing general mathematical skills and strategies?

5.3. Standardizing Computational Methods

When the secondary teacher looks at computational work done by the members of a first-year class, newly arrived from their primary schools, he usually finds several different procedures and methods of setting out being used. How should he react? Is it reasonable, *from the child's point of view*, to attempt to impose uniformity? If he should decide to insist that everyone does subtraction by "decomposition of the top number", what of the pupils who are confident subtractors using the "equal additions" method?

Can the variety of pupil's methods be exploited in a positive way? The realization on the pupil's part that *his* method of subtraction is not the only one is probably a very important experience. Perhaps even more important is the knowledge that all valid methods are right ones and their validity is not dependent on the views of the teacher.

Has the teacher a case for making things easier for himself by attempting to standardize certain operations? Are all these ways of setting out 17×39 acceptable, or should they all be reduced to the first? (I myself was taught the third—it has *some* advantages!)

$$
\begin{array}{ccc}
39 & 39 & 39 \\
17 & 17 & 17 \\
\hline
390 & 273 & 39 \\
273 & 39 & 273 \\
\hline
663 & 663 & 663
\end{array}
$$

In the case of $32{\cdot}5 \times 0{\cdot}0024$, should he teach a standardized method of locating the decimal point? If so, which one? There are at least three—working with $3{\cdot}25 \times 0{\cdot}024$ and lining up the units; working with 325×24 and counting the decimal places; working with $3{\cdot}25 \times 10^1 \times 2{\cdot}4 \times 10^{-3}$—and this is a case where the most foolproof method is probably the one which is hardest to explain.

Are there long-term benefits to be reaped from the more imaginative but riskier procedure of introducing a wide choice of methods for discussion and consideration? For example, subtraction:

(a) by decomposition of the top

$$
\begin{array}{c}
\overset{1}{5}2 \\
29 \\
\hline
23
\end{array}
\left(= \begin{array}{cc} 40 & 12 \\ 20 & 9 \\ \hline 20 & 3 \end{array} \right)
$$

(b) by equal additions to top and bottom

$$
\begin{array}{c}
52 \\
\underset{1}{2}9 \\
\hline
23
\end{array}
\left(= \begin{array}{cc} 50 & 12 \\ 30 & 9 \\ \hline 20 & 3 \end{array} \right)
$$

(c) by reversing addition: set out

$$
\begin{array}{c}
29 \\
\\
\hline
52
\end{array}
\quad \text{and fill in} \quad
\begin{array}{c}
29 \\
3 \\
23 \\
\hline
52
\end{array}
$$

$$
\left(= \begin{array}{cc} 29 & 32 \\ 3 & 20 \\ \hline 32 & 52 \end{array} \right)
$$

(d) by complementing to 9
$$
\left(\begin{array}{l} 52 - 29 = 52 + 70 - 99 \\ \quad\quad\quad = 52 + 70 + 1 - 100 \end{array} \right)
$$

$$
\begin{array}{c}
52 \\
70 \\
\hline
122 \\
\searrow 1 \\
23
\end{array}
$$

Thus:
$$
\begin{array}{c}
764 \\
387 \\
\end{array}
\quad \text{write} \quad
\begin{array}{c}
764 \\
+612 \quad \text{(nines complement of 387)} \\
\hline
1376 \\
\searrow 1 \quad \text{``end-around carry''} \\
\hline
377
\end{array}
$$

This last method is often used in the internal logic of a computer. Its justification is an interesting exercise.

Again the method of multiplication by repeated halving and doubling (sometimes attributed to Russian peasants) has interesting links with binary notation:

$$
\begin{array}{cc}
29 \times 21 \\
58 & 10 \\
116 & 5 \\
\cancel{232} & 2 \\
464 & 1 \\
\hline
609
\end{array}
$$

We add up only those numbers where the figure in the second column is *odd*. In effect, we multiply 29 by the binary number $10101 (= 16 + 4 + 1)$.

Ultimately the teacher has to guide each pupil to some method which will be standard for himself, so that he can use it accurately, confidently and without thinking. This may not be the method he practises on arrival at secondary school, if that method is inefficient (e.g. $290 \div 13$ by repeated subtraction of 13 in the units) or inaccurate. But equally it need not be the same as that of other members of the class.

5.4. The Number-Line

Before any systematic work can be undertaken on directed numbers or fractions it will almost certainly be necessary to review the knowledge and experience of the pupils with the four rules applied to the whole numbers $W = \{0, 1, 2, 3, \ldots\}$. A good way of doing this is to relate everything to the number-line, which should be prominently displayed in the classroom.

It is strongly recommended that the number-line should be described as having an *origin* (corresponding to 0—the starting point), a chosen unit of length and a chosen positive direction indicated by an arrow-head, so that the number 1 is marked at the point at one unit distance from the origin in the arrow-head direction.

Addition of natural numbers (or whole numbers, if W is used) is illustrated by vector addition of directed steps on the number-line with the appropriate measures, the first step starting from 0, the second step starting from the end point of the first step, etc.; e.g.

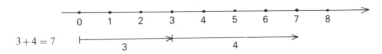

A useful way of thinking is being built up that will carry over to integers, rationals, etc.

The teacher needs to be clear in his own mind about the step which is being taken when this is done, whether or not he thinks it wise to make it explicit to the pupils. They may well have learnt about addition in two ways:

(*a*) By putting together two (counted) collections of objects, and "counting on" to get the total as illustrated below:

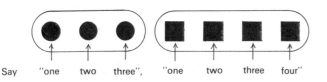

Say   "one   two   three",   "one   two   three   four"

Add to get

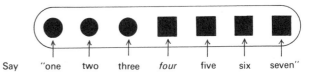

Say   "one   two   three   *four*   five   six   seven"

Here we match the objects to a memorized set of number names, and we add by counting on the new set, beginning from where we left off.

(*b*) By putting end-to-end as a "3-rod" of length 3 and a "4-rod" of length 4, finally matching the two to a "7-rod" of length 7.

All pupils should be familiar from primary school with the fact that these two methods give the same result, but in one case the numbers are derived from matching sets (so-called *cardinal* numbers) and in the other they are one-dimensional vectors represented by lengths. In more sophisticated terms, these systems are *isomorphic*, i.e. they have precisely the same structure, but the second leads on more easily to the various extensions of the counting numbers.

Should the difference be pointed out, and should a formal definition of either type of number be given? Opinions differ, but most agree that formal definitions should not be given to children at this stage (see, e.g. *Mathematics Begins*, p. 43, *Nuffield Maths Project* 1). Some kind of explanation may, however, be necessary for the pupil who asks whether we are adding the *points* on the number-line or who tries to locate (perhaps even to write) the numbers in the *spaces* between the points; we are in fact adding the labels of the points by adding the lengths of the spaces between them and the zero, and our justification for this procedure is that it works, i.e. the two systems are isomorphic. Probably the moment to draw attention to this is when we want to introduce negative shifts; the meaning of 3, $^+3$, $^-3$ then call for explanation, which is best given by numerous examples as recommended below.

Subtraction. The point about subtraction which it is essential to establish for further development is that the questions: "What is left if 4 is taken from 7?" (or the result of "7 take away 4") and "What must we add to 4 to get 7?" are the same. Here again an approach by examples leads to a diagram:

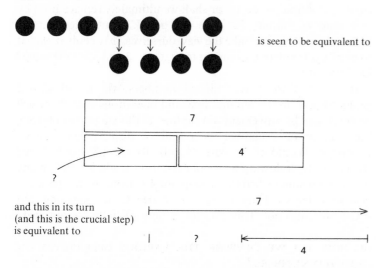

is seen to be equivalent to

and this in its turn
(and this is the crucial step)
is equivalent to

Seven steps to the right and four steps to the left on the number-line then leads at once to $7-4 = {}^+7 + {}^-4$ (if this notation is introduced) and we have the important link with algebra that

$$7-4 = x \quad \text{is equivalent to} \quad 7 = x+4.$$

Multiplication on the number-line is a mixed affair. "Three times four" (which seems to be the more normal reading of 3×4, which ought strictly to mean "three multiplied by four", i.e. four times three) can as yet only be taken to mean "a step of 4 repeated 3 times", i.e. $4+4+4$. The 4 has a geometrical picture but the 3 does not. To give it one, we need the familiar two-dimensional multiplication table, and there is a source of confusion here, since traditionally the numbers go in the cells and not (as on the number-line) at the boundary-points.

All pupils will, as a result of their experiences, readily assent to such facts as $3 \times 4 = 4 \times 3$; these are easily demonstrated by counting dots in rectangular arrays, but they are not obvious from the number-line and cannot at this stage be made so.

Division presents similar difficulties; indeed rather more, because three different types of question are involved.

(a) I have 50 apples and I want to give 3 to each child at a party; how many children can I manage to do this for?

(b) I have 50 kg of flour to distribute equally among 3 people; how much will each get?

(c) I have 50 sacks of fertilizer; on the sack it says that 3 sacks will cover 1 hectare; how many hectares can I cover?

Of these (a) is just repeated subtraction and can be demonstrated on a number-line; (b) cannot be tackled this way without a preliminary "definition" of a unit of 3 kg as a "deal-out" of 1 kg each. Any attempt to do this by repeated subtraction of 3s will result in confusion as to whether what is left over is people or flour or kg weights. (c) of course is a "proportion sum"; the idea of ratio is involved and the answer is a rational number.

(a) is easiest and can be tackled practically in a variety of ways of which the number-line is one; (b) really does involve "division into parts" and involves the conversion of at least some of the flour into $\frac{1}{3}$-kg bags; (c) is asking "What number must we multiply 3 by to get 50?" and is equivalent to solving $50:3 = x:1$ or $3x = 50$.

The first approaches to such problems may well have been made in primary school. The way forward is through generalization from examples in which the use of algebra is becoming important, especially in the step from (*b*) to (*c*). The use of the slide rule as a "proportionalizer" (see 7.4) is helpful here. It is suggested that work of this kind should lead into, rather than arise from, any formal treatment of rational numbers. There is obviously a wide area of discussion here, and a useful occasion for departmental (and inter-departmental) collaboration and decision-making.

5.5. Introducing Directed Numbers

(a) WHAT CONCRETE EXPERIENCE OF NEGATIVE QUANTITIES ARE PUPILS LIKELY TO HAVE?

Assuming that directed numbers are likely to arise first in connection with practical needs—which may be an algebraic need, like that of finding a formula to convert Celsius to Fahrenheit on a temperature scale—we have to ask what experience we can draw on and extend. Besides the obvious example of the temperature scale, the pupils are likely to have met negative numbers, or to have experienced the need for them, in various other practical situations; for example:

(1) Distances to the north from the equator positive; distances to the south negative (or similarly, east and west).
(2) Levels in feet above sea-level positive, levels in feet below sea-level negative.
(3) On a flight of stairs: steps up, positive; steps down, negative.
(4) Starting at a point on a circle: rotations in one direction, positive; rotations in the opposite direction, negative.
(5) Profit taken as positive and loss as negative.

In these examples of integers, the pupil is introduced to addition, subtraction and ordering, while multiplication and division will not arise until a later stage.

(b) WHAT CONCEPT OF A DIRECTED NUMBER WILL PREDOMINATE IN THE EARLY STAGES?

If we start with a temperature scale, it is natural to locate the signed numbers as *points* on the scale, but then it is unnatural to operate with them. What physical process corresponds to *adding* a temperature of $^-4°C$ to one of $^+10°C$? On the other hand it may be difficult to introduce the idea of numbers as *shifts* unless we have previously thought of them in this way. (Hence the discussion of 5.3.) If both ideas are introduced, how are they going to be reconciled? Will it confuse the pupil or help to clarify his thinking if we distinguish the number $^-3$ ("negative 3") from the operation -3 ("take away 3") by word and symbol? If we do so at the start, shall we continue to do so, or shall we ultimately replace both by -3, read as "minus 3"? Has $\bar{3}$ ("bar 3") any place outside logarithms? Do we (*a*) take the view ourselves, (*b*) openly preach it to pupils, (*c*) explain the reasons for it, that $^+3$ and 3 are the same? Or different?

It seems obvious that signed numbers will be illustrated geometrically on the number-line, and operations with them will be developed by movements on the line; at this stage, if not before, the concept of a number as a shift or displacement will be necessary. Would it be wise to talk to the physicists here? (Incidentally, following a recommendation made in 1962, many physicists distinguished the scale-point 4°C from the temperature *change* 4 deg C. Thus 4 deg $C + ^-6$ deg C has meaning, but $4°C + ^-6°C$ has not. This notation is now officially discouraged.)

(c) HOW DO WE DEVELOP THE VARIOUS OPERATIONS ON DIRECTED NUMBERS?

Do we introduce all four in quick succession, or delay × and ÷ as being more abstract and difficult to explain? Do we confine operations at first to integers (*Z*) or do we introduce directed rationals as well?

Addition can be demonstrated by taking successive steps along the number-line, starting at 0. Thus $^+3 + {}^-7$ means "start at 0, take 3 positive steps (to the right, usually) and *then* 7 negative steps; where do you end up?" But how about subtraction? There are two main approaches to $a - b$. The first asks "what must we add to b to get a" and leads to the idea of the *displacement from b to a*. This is very important later on (**BA** $= \mathbf{a} - \mathbf{b}$) but is it a difficult idea for our pupils? The other way is by means of *additive inverses*; $a - b = a + ({}^-b)$ where ^-b is the shift which *undoes* the work of the shift b. Thus $^-(^+2)$ is $^-2$ and $^-(^-2)$ is $^+2$.

If we adopt this second method, do we have to use the notation (or any other special notation) to get across the idea?

In view of the importance of each idea, should we use both approaches and show that they lead to the same results, or will this confuse our weaker pupils?

(d) MULTIPLICATION

This involves problems. As hinted above, we may skate over the difficulties of $^-3 \times 2$ ("negative 3 times 2") by insisting that it must be the same as $2 \times {}^-3 =$ two shifts of negative $3 = {}^-6$. This is easily shown on the number-line:

This defines multiplication as repeated addition, and will not help us with $^-2 \times {}^-3$. We can only give a meaning to this by appealing to the structure which we want the directed numbers to have. The following argument is presented in *Modern Mathematics for Schools*:

$$^-2 \times {}^-3 + {}^+2 \times {}^-3 = ({}^-2 + {}^+2) \times {}^-3 \quad \text{distributive law}$$
$$= 0 \times {}^-3$$
$$= 0 \quad \text{(this again depends on the distributive law, or by analogy from } W)$$

Accordingly $^-2 \times {}^-3 + {}^-6 = 0$, so that
$\qquad ^-2 \times {}^-3$ is the additive inverse of $^-6$, which is $^+6$.

At what stage, if at all, will such a "proof" be given to pupils? Will it be convincing? What other approaches are possible?

A number of approaches have been devised.

(1) We can identify the operation $\times {}^-1$ with that of taking the additive inverse. This is plausible, since $^-1 \times 2 = 2 \times {}^-1 = {}^-2$ and so on. If we like, and our geometric activities invite it, we can identify this with a half-turn about O, or an enlargement with scale-factor $^-1$.

We then have $^-2 \times {}^-3 = (2 \times {}^-1) \times {}^-3 = 2 \times ({}^-1 \times {}^-3)$ (note the use of the associative law) $= 2 \times {}^+3 = {}^+6$.

(2) We can use number patterns:

2×3	2	1	0	$^-1$	$^-2$	$^-3$
6	4	2	0	$^-2$	$^-4$	$^-6$

: each step is a subtraction of 2

$^-2 \times 3$	2	1	0	$^-1$	$^-2$	$^-3$
-6	-4	-2	0	?	?	?

each step is an addition of 2

The table can be completed by observing the pattern.

(3) We can use algebraic ideas:

$$(5-3) \times (5-2) = 2 \times 3 = 6$$
$$(5-3) \times (5-2) = 5 \times 5 - 3 \times 5 - 5 \times 2 + (-3) \times (-2)$$
$$\text{so that} \quad 6 = 25 - 15 - 10 + (-3) \times (-2)$$
$$\text{and} \quad (-3) \times (-2) = 6.$$

Of course in all these approaches the basic structure of Z has been smuggled in somewhere. Is it better, as some contend, to "come clean" and declare openly what we are doing? If so, the declaration will need very careful preparation.

(e) THE PUPILS' VIEWPOINT

Is precision the same as communication?

Is explanation the same as conviction?

Will most pupils not revert to saying "minus times minus is plus" and regard all the rest as meaningless mumbo-jumbo? How much will they lose if they do?

Is there a case for confining the use of directed numbers for slower learners to simple examples of addition and subtraction of integers?

If we try to induce pupils to discover and formulate rules of procedure for themselves by guided exercises and experiment with patterns, what of the pupil who says "Why don't you just tell me the answer instead of wasting all this time?"

5.6. Introducing Rational Numbers

The problems here and the questions to be discussed are very similar to those in section 5, but there are some features which call for special mention.

(a) THE NOTATION

Fractions are familiar to children in many contexts; if their rulers are not actually marked with signs such as $\frac{1}{2}, \frac{1}{4}, \frac{1}{16}$, some of these are common on road signs and signposts "Services $\frac{1}{2}$ mile", "Little Pugwash $\frac{3}{4}$". In modern signs the solidus (/) is invariably omitted; do children notice this? Only the commoner fractions $\frac{1}{4}, \frac{1}{2}, \frac{3}{4}$, and occasionally $\frac{1}{3}, \frac{2}{3}$, occur in this way, but the notation becomes familiar before its *raison d'être*. Many books take it for granted, e.g.

> One third of a whole is written $\frac{1}{3}$ of a whole, the notation $\frac{1}{3}$ being used to indicate that the whole is divided into three parts and we take one of these.

Many pupils find this sudden appearance of $\frac{1}{3}$ difficult to grasp and probably accept it simply from constant usage. The ideas to be assimilated seem to be:

(i) $\frac{1}{3}$ is the same as $1 \div 3$ and means what we get when we divide a unit (a length, a cake, an area...) into 3 equal parts.

(ii) $\frac{2}{3}$ is $2 \times \frac{1}{3}$ and also $2 \div 3$ and can be thought of either as two "thirds" or as a third of 2. Both of these can be illustrated in two ways: on the number-line

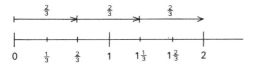

or by cutting up areas:

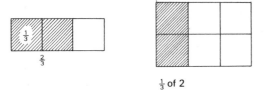

$\frac{1}{3}$ of 2

The number-line approach may be confusing if it has not already become familiar through the integers.

(b) EQUIVALENT FRACTIONS

The all-important idea which it is essential to get across is that fractions like $\frac{2}{3}, \frac{4}{6}, \frac{6}{9}, \ldots$ represent the same number. Here again the two models can both help:

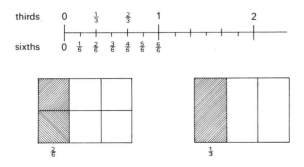

Another device which is very useful for this and a great many other purposes is the representation of fractions on squared paper, p/q

being represented by the point (q, p). (See, for example, *SMP Book B*, chapter 5.)

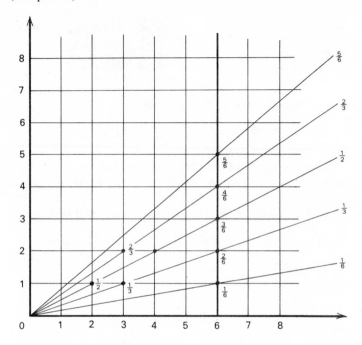

In this useful model, equivalent (or equal) fractions are represented by the lattice points with positive coordinates that lie on a straight line through the origin, the gradient of the line being in each case the corresponding rational number; e.g. the line of gradient $\frac{1}{2}$ passes through the lattice points $(2, 1)$, $(4, 2)$, $(6, 3)$, $(8, 4), \ldots$, illustrating the equalities $\frac{1}{2} = \frac{2}{4} = \frac{3}{6} = \frac{4}{8} = \ldots$. Fractions can then be added or subtracted by finding a suitable vertical line to use as the number-line, e.g.

$$\tfrac{1}{2} - \tfrac{1}{3} = \tfrac{3}{6} - \tfrac{2}{6} = \tfrac{1}{6}$$

Fractions can also be compared by comparing the slopes of their lines; if the line for $\frac{4}{5}$ is drawn, it will be seen to be less steep than that for $\frac{5}{6}$, so $\frac{4}{5} < \frac{5}{6}$.

(c) OPERATIONS WITH FRACTIONS

To add or subtract fractions we can again use the number-line, but we can only measure the result if we use a small enough division of the units. We are brought back to the idea of equivalent fractions and being able to add (by counting on) fractions of the same kind—hence, incidentally, the word "denominator" which *names the kind* of fraction, while "numerator" *counts how many*. To add $\frac{1}{3}$ and $\frac{3}{4}$ we must choose a kind of subdivision in which both can be represented—in the plane model, a vertical number-line on which both sloping lines have dots (diagrams below and on page 58).

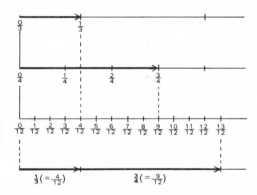

$$\tfrac{1}{3} + \tfrac{3}{4} = \tfrac{4}{12} + \tfrac{9}{12} = \tfrac{13}{12} = 1\tfrac{1}{12}$$

Here we need either the idea of LCM, or we can use the product of the denominators. For example,

$$\frac{3}{4} + \frac{5}{6} = \frac{3 \times 6}{4 \times 6} + \frac{4 \times 5}{4 \times 6} = \frac{18}{24} + \frac{20}{24} = \frac{38}{24} = \frac{19}{12}$$

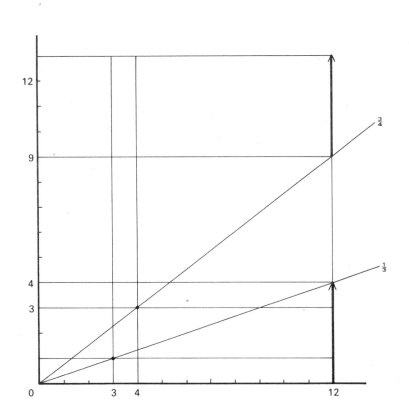

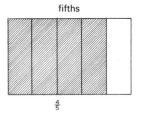

fifths

$\frac{4}{5}$

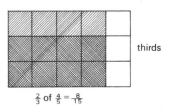

thirds

$\frac{2}{3}$ of $\frac{4}{5} = \frac{8}{15}$

It may or may not help to spell this out as

$$\frac{2}{3} \times \frac{4}{5} = 2 \times \frac{1}{3} \times \frac{4}{5} = 2 \times \frac{1}{3} \text{ of } \frac{3 \times 4}{3 \times 5} = 2 \times \frac{4}{3 \times 5} = \frac{2 \times 4}{3 \times 5} = \frac{8}{15}.$$

These steps spell out in symbolism what has been done in the diagram—or could be done practically using squared paper and scissors.

Division is probably by this time best approached as the inverse of multiplication; e.g. to find $\frac{5}{6} \div \frac{3}{4}$ we have to find $\frac{x}{y}$ so that $\frac{x}{y} \times \frac{3}{4} = \frac{5}{6}$, which gives

$$\frac{x}{4y} \times 3 = \frac{5}{6} = \frac{5 \times 3}{6 \times 3} = \frac{5}{18} \times 3$$

so that

$$\frac{x}{4y} = \frac{5}{18} = \frac{4 \times 5}{4 \times 18} = \frac{1}{4} \text{ of } \frac{4 \times 5}{18}$$

giving finally

$$\frac{x}{y} = \frac{4 \times 5}{18} = \frac{4 \times 5}{3 \times 6}$$

It needs a long demonstration to make this formal procedure plausible in either model, but the rule can be approached through simpler cases. Alternatively, the "multiplicative inverse" idea can be used if the ideas of neutral elements and inverses are familiar

Multiplication can be demonstrated best by cutting up areas—once again, the number-line is not the most satisfactory approach, but it can be used at a second stage. For example, to show $\frac{2}{3} \times \frac{4}{5}$ (assuming this means "take two-thirds of $\frac{4}{5}$") we proceed as the diagram indicates already, but to introduce them for this purpose alone is probably unwise.

(d) HOW FAR DO WE GO?

The same questions need to be asked here as were asked before, but there is an additional factor to be taken into account. In applications of mathematics the use of ratio and proportion is all-pervasive. Facility and assurance in handling these topics pre-supposes a sound grasp of the rules for multiplying fractions and the concept of equivalence. Ought we therefore to proceed by means of algebra as rapidly as possible to the rule:

$$\frac{a}{b} = \frac{c}{d} \quad \Leftrightarrow \quad ad = bc$$

and teach its usefulness in applications? Once again, a ripe field for discussion.

425 g of SOPO for 56p, or 750 g for £1 (special offer): which is the better buy?

Ought we to make it our aim that all our pupils could give an answer, with or without an electronic calculator?

5.7. Conclusion

This chapter has raised more questions than it answers—deliberately, because there is no generally applicable, still less any "official", answer to any of them. Everything depends on the needs, past experience, present attitude and future aspirations of the pupils concerned. But in seeking to answer some of these questions the teacher will find himself confronted by a deeper one: what am I trying to teach this *for*? Reconsideration of the objectives listed in chapter 1 is therefore required, and their applicability to the situation under discussion.

There are always two challenges confronting the conscientious teacher of mathematics: to enable his pupils to achieve sufficient skill in the use of mathematics as a tool to cope with the demands of other subjects and, later on, with the demands of life in a technological world; and to open their eyes and fire their imaginations with the beauty and power of mathematics as an achievement of the rational human mind. We hope that in answering the questions posed by this chapter the two will be not incompatible.

6 Number in Applications

6.0. Introduction

Mathematics is used today in a wide variety of fields. "Applied mathematics" has traditionally been associated with physics and chemistry, and mathematics of a rather different kind has been needed for accountancy and actuarial work. But increasingly the life sciences such as biology and psychology, geography and economics have become heavily dependent on mathematical ideas, and even such supposedly non-mathematical studies as music and literature have not been unaffected. Statistics has applications in every area of human activity, and the computer, designed on logical and mathematical principles, can be set to perform many at first sight non-mathematical tasks.

These varied fields of study require equally varied mathematical tools for the solution of their problems, many of them newly devised for specific purposes, but all relying on a basic appreciation of number. Of course, no pupil can be expected to be familiar with the technical terminology of so wide a range of subjects, not even with those that find a place in the school curriculum; we shall concentrate here on a few matters which seem to be central to the various applications of mathematics and which may cause difficulties in correlating the mathematics teaching with the needs of other subjects. A fuller discussion is to be found in the book in the present series: *Mathematics across the Curriculum.*

6.1. Scientific Notation, Large and Small Numbers

In all modern syllabuses *scientific notation* for numbers is defined, namely $x \times 10^a$, where $1 \leqslant x < 10$ and a is an integer, and practice given in the use of this notation. The term *standard form* is often used instead of *scientific notation*, but the latter is preferred

by teachers of physics and chemistry. Many pupils are interested in the varied collection of numbers, large and small, that can be obtained from lists of facts about topics in physics, chemistry, astronomy, etc. For example, from *Inequalities and Optimal Problems in Mathematics and the Sciences* by G. Stephenson (Longman, 1971) we have:

Space Scale

Radius of visible universe	10^{23} km
Distance of nearest galaxy	10^{19} km
Distance of nearest star	10^{14} km
Distance of sun	$1 \cdot 5 \times 10^8$ km
Distance of moon	$4 \cdot 0 \times 10^5$ km
Highest mountains on earth	$8 \cdot 8$ km
Human dimensions	2 m
Atomic radius	10^{-8} cm
Nuclear radius	10^{-13} cm

Time Scale

Galaxies and universe formed	10^5 million years ago
Solar system formed	10^4 million years ago
Earth formed	$4 \cdot 5 \times 10^3$ million years ago
Micro fossils formed	$3 \cdot 2 \times 10^3$ million years ago
Marine evolution	6×10^2 million years ago
Dinosaurs in existence	2×10^2 million years ago
Early man evolved	4 to 1 million years ago
Early civilization began	10^4 years ago.

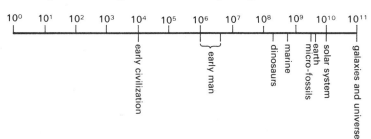

Pupils are likely to meet scales like this time scale long before they meet the ideas of logarithms, and it can help them to understand the use of indices well before they need to do any manipulation with them. In the diagram above, teachers can emphasize that each gap means "ten times as long ago".

Information (and use of numbers) of this kind is almost limitless, e.g. mean radius and mass of the sun, earth, moon; mean free path of molecules for air, argon, hydrogen, etc.; velocity of light, sound, etc.; miscellaneous constants such as Avogadro's number, gas constant, Boltzmann's constant; numbers associated with the many records appearing in volumes such as the *Encyclopaedia Britannica* and the *Guinness Book of Records*.

6.2. Ratio and Proportion

The work associated with ratio and proportion appears in many applications. In number work in mathematics teaching we tend to restrict numbers to integers or rational numbers when ratio and proportion are first introduced. This is necessary since the intervention of numerical difficulties would add greatly to the already difficult task of presenting the concepts. Later we return to the concepts with heavier numerical manipulation when the slide rule, log tables or other aids to calculation become available. Unfortunately many users of mathematics want the ideas of ratio and proportion with decimals to several places at a relatively early stage. Cooperation between such a user and the mathematics teacher might help; on the whole the main users involved are those in physics, chemistry and engineering. A formula such as $R = V/I$ might lead to (or arise from) an experiment in which R is a constant and its value is being determined by a number of readings which give rise to ratios $V_1/I_1, V_2/I_2, \ldots, V_n/I_n$ (for some n), with the V_i, I_i as numbers in terms of certain measures. Graphical fitting of a line to plotted points is normally used for this type of activity; in this case, using the points (I_i, V_i), we are estimating the gradient of the fitted line. In another situation the user might want $V_1/I_1 = V_2/I$ in

which V_1, V_2, I_1 have given numerical values and I has to be determined. Clearly mathematics teaching ought to cope with such situations. On the other hand there are empirical formulae that are much more difficult to handle, e.g. the following "ratio type" formula for gaseous volumes:

$$\frac{v_0}{v} = \frac{p}{760(1 + 0.00367t)}$$

where p denotes pressure in mm of Hg (or torr) and t temperature in °C. It is almost certainly true that many users do not appreciate the difficulties involved in preparing pupils to cope with such complications, even when only numerical work is involved.

Another simple example of use of ratios arises in music with musical scales:

	C	D	E	F	G	A	B	C	
Vibration ratios	24	27	30	32	36	40	45	48	} basic (i.e. diatonic) scale
	1·000	1·125	1·250	1·333	1·500	1·667	1·875	2·000	
Intervals	$\frac{9}{8}$	$\frac{10}{9}$	$\frac{16}{15}$	$\frac{9}{8}$	$\frac{10}{9}$	$\frac{9}{8}$	$\frac{16}{15}$		

The vibration numbers in the Diatonic Scale must bear the given ratios to each other, but their absolute values are a matter of convention. The pitch of "middle C" is often taken at different values for different purposes (e.g. at 261, 273 or 256).

In the *SMP* numbered course, considerable emphasis is placed on ratio and proportion, and new language is used which requires some explanation. To make the ideas clearer, especially for weaker pupils, the writers regard ratio and proportion from two points of view, using *scale factors* and *multipliers*. We illustrate these in the following example:

Example. If a single meal costs £1·50, then the total cost of meals for 10, 15, 25 and 40 people are £15, £22·50, £37·50 and £60 respectively.

SCALE FACTORS

The set of numbers of people 10, 15, 25, 40 and the set of total costs £15, £22·50, £37·50, £60 are *proportional sets* (*SMP Y*, p. 95).

We can decide whether two (ordered) sets are proportional by calculating the *scale factors* or by calculating the *multipliers for each set*. When two sets are proportional, we shall write $10:15:25:40 = 15:22 \cdot 5:37 \cdot 5:60$.

To calculate the *scale factors*, we take the corresponding pairs of elements from the sets and divide. These sets are *proportional* since the *scale factor* is constant.

$$
\begin{array}{cccc}
10 & 15 & 25 & 40 \\
\downarrow\frac{3}{2} & \downarrow\frac{3}{2} & \downarrow\frac{3}{2} & \downarrow\frac{3}{2} \quad \text{SCALE FACTOR} = \tfrac{3}{2} \\
15 & 22 \cdot 5 & 37 \cdot 5 & 60
\end{array}
$$

This scale factor gives the ratio $3:2$ for the proportional sets, and the ratio $3:2$ has an associated fraction $\frac{3}{2}$. Since the ratios are equal for the elements of the set, so are the scale factors.

The advantage of calculating scale factors becomes more apparent when we draw a graph for the two sets. The scale factor is the gradient of the line joining the origin to the point on the graph. Thus equal scale factors means equal gradients, and so proportional sets give a straight-line graph through the origin.

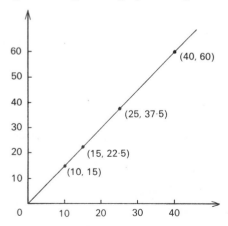

This language can be used to check whether we have a linear function or not. A function is linear if its *difference sets* are

proportional sets, and the constant scale factor for these sets is the gradient of its graph, e.g.

X	10	17	21	30
Y	26	40	48	66

gives a linear graph since

$$
\begin{array}{lcccc}
X \text{ differences} & 7 & 4 & 9 & \\
 & \downarrow 2 & \downarrow 2 & \downarrow 2 & \text{(SCALE FACTOR)} \\
Y \text{ differences} & 14 & 8 & 18 &
\end{array}
$$

has a constant scale factor 2. The gradient of the linear graph is 2.

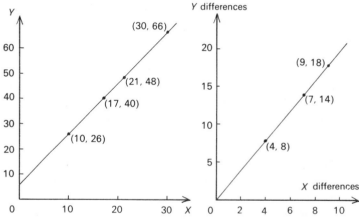

SMP uses the words *scale factor* to link different branches of mathematics. It is introduced in *Book D* (p. 26) in a geometrical sense, used for trigonometry in *Book G* (p. 78) and then arithmetically for proportional sets in *Book Y* (p. 95). The scale factor is a most useful idea, for it is the common concept in such quantities as gradient, velocity and resistance.

MULTIPLIERS

Returning to the example above, in order to calculate the *multipliers* for each set, we take adjacent elements and divide.

Thus

and the set of multipliers is $\{\frac{3}{2}, \frac{5}{3}, \frac{8}{5}\}$. Similarly the set $\{15, 22\cdot5, 37\cdot5, 60\}$ also has as multipliers the ordered set $\{\frac{3}{2}, \frac{5}{3}, \frac{8}{5}\}$. (See *SMP Book Y*, p. 61.)

An advantage in using the set of multipliers is that, as the quotients of quantities with the same units, the multipliers are pure numbers, i.e. they are unit-free.

Multipliers appear again for "direct" proportionality in the unitary method. Thus

If 15 men pay £22·5,
then 25 men pay £22·5 $\times \frac{25}{15}$,
where $\frac{25}{15}$ is the multiplier.

To conclude, we need scale factors and multipliers in different situations, and pupils will only be able to apply the "ratio and proportion" ideas well if they have both words available. The applications to resistance above are best described in terms of the scale factor, which in this case actually is the resistance. It is a pleasant feature of the scale factor that it is often recognizable as a concept that has already been named. On the other hand multipliers are useful to describe the diatonic scale, and we can make remarks such as the following by using the language of multipliers:

If middle C is 271 c/s, then the C above middle C is 271 × 2 = 542 c/s.

2 is the multiplier; the use of the word *multiplier* enables us to describe a calculation more explicitly. It is a pity that these words are used, in an arithmetical sense, rather late in the *SMP* lettered course. In fact, proportion is almost excluded from the *SMP* CSE course, but the ideas appear in *Books 2* and *4* of the "O" Level course, as well as in *Book Y*. This reflects the views of many

teachers of mathematics that proportion is a rather more difficult idea than many of its users suppose. This is probably because when it is said (for example) that *i* is proportional to *V*, *i* and *V* are not now particular unknown quantities to be determined, but representatives of two sets of corresponding quantities in a particular experiment; the idea of functional dependence is involved, and of two things being allowed to vary while other things are kept constant.

6.3. Measurement and Approximations

A common process in measurement is to take a sequence of approximations by decimals.

> *Example.* We might say that the length of a rod is 12 cm. When we look more closely, we see that the 12-cm mark does not exactly correspond with the end of the rod, and so, by dividing each cm into parts, we might go on to say that its length is between 12·1 cm and 12·2 cm, and so on.

In making such measurements, we can gain insight into the existence of irrational numbers. In the same way as we decide whether each decimal is too large or too small for a measured length, we can decide whether each *rational number* is larger or smaller than a given *irrational number*, and an irrational number arises in any process in which every rational number is either too large or else too small.

We now consider some lessons in which the approximations to the irrational are allocated to the upper class and the lower class according as to whether it is found to be larger or smaller than the number sought.

LESSON 1 (A teacher's account)

(This le son is also described in an article by D. S. Hale in *Mathematics Teaching* 67, June 1974.)

> A third-year class were doing some examples about the volumes of similar shapes. In the course of a conversation with two boys who had finished,

suggested that they might think about the problem of designing a paint tin which would hold twice as much paint as a given tin: the two tins were to be of similar shape.

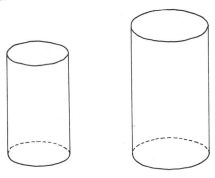

There was an immediate response by one of the boys: "You make the dimensions $1\frac{1}{2}$ times as big." We tested this suggestion.

$$1\tfrac{1}{2} \times 1\tfrac{1}{2} \times 1\tfrac{1}{2} = \tfrac{27}{8}$$

Too big. The larger tin would hold more than three times the smaller tin. "What about $1\frac{1}{4}$" suggested the other boy. So we worked out

$$1\tfrac{1}{4} \times 1\tfrac{1}{4} \times 1\tfrac{1}{4} = \tfrac{125}{64}$$

Better, but now the result was just too small. The next suggestion was $1\frac{3}{8}$ and, with some difficulty, we obtained

$$1\tfrac{3}{8} \times 1\tfrac{3}{8} \times 1\tfrac{3}{8} = \tfrac{1331}{512}$$

which was clearly too large.

At this stage there was a lengthy pause which ended with the suggestion that it must be larger than 5/4, perhaps (5·1)/4. By now the bell was ringing for the end of the period, so there was no time to test the latest conjecture; in any case, there was no calculator available. I did, however, have time to ask: "Do you think we would find an exact answer if we searched long enough?" "Yes", they both replied confidently.

The next lesson comes from an article in *Mathematics Teaching* 63, June 1973, "Approximating by Vectors", by T. J. Fletcher.

LESSON 2

To calculate $\sqrt{2}$ by using a series of approximations by fractions.

To calculate $\sqrt{2}$ we start with $(1, 1)$ and $(1, 2)$ since

$$\tfrac{1}{1} < \sqrt{2} < \tfrac{2}{1}.$$

We now take the *mediant* of these fractions, i.e. $\dfrac{1+2}{1+1}$, for a new approximation; $\dfrac{1+2}{1+1} = \dfrac{3}{2}$, which will be between $\dfrac{1}{1}$ and $\dfrac{2}{1}$.

Now $(\tfrac{3}{2})^2 = \tfrac{9}{4} > 2$ and so

$$\tfrac{1}{1} < \sqrt{2} < \tfrac{3}{2}.$$

The next approximation is $\dfrac{1+3}{1+2} = \dfrac{4}{3}$, $\left(\dfrac{4}{3}\right)^2 = \dfrac{16}{9} < 2$ and so

$$\tfrac{4}{3} < \sqrt{2} < \tfrac{3}{2}.$$

Carrying on with this process, we obtain the chain of inequalities

$$\tfrac{1}{1} < \tfrac{4}{3} < \tfrac{7}{5} < \tfrac{24}{17} < \ldots \sqrt{2} \ldots < \tfrac{17}{12} < \tfrac{10}{7} < \tfrac{3}{2} < \tfrac{2}{1}.$$

By calculating these rational numbers we have a fairly accurate value of $\sqrt{2}$. Since

$$1\cdot411 < \tfrac{24}{1\cdot} \quad \text{and} \quad \tfrac{17}{12} < 1\cdot417.$$

we have

$$1.41 < \sqrt{2} < 1\cdot42.$$

Fletcher goes on to give a series of approximations for further irrationals $\sqrt[3]{2}$, $\sqrt[10]{10}$, $\sqrt[12]{2}$ and $\log_{10}2$.

In the lessons above, the pupils are getting approximations through a series of inequalities. It is also interesting to look at behaviour close to a number which is known, as for example in the problem described on page 78, of finding the volumes of open boxes formed by cutting equal corners from a sheet of metal 15 cm square.

The maximum volume was found to occur when the corners removed were of side 2·5 cm; to convince themselves of this the class found it necessary to take numbers very close to 2·5 and see what happened to the volume.

Knowledge of the rationals and irrationals may be gained in this informal way. Further examples may be found in another book in this series *The Mathematics Curriculum: From Graphs to Calculus*.

6.4. Some Difficulties with New Syllabuses*

This chapter has drawn attention to some new language and methods in mathematics courses, which have not always been welcomed by science teachers. New methods always take time to be assimilated, but science teachers have experienced particular difficulties owing to these changes. They have not been clear about the reasons for change, and the timing of the introduction of topics has sometimes been arranged without reference to the implications for other subjects. Some teachers stress the role of mathematics as a service subject, while others emphasize that a modern mathematics course should justify its own usefulness, but whichever view we take of the role of mathematics, we should accept that there has been a degree of mismatch in new courses.

Some of the difficulties are quite trivial; some can be thrashed out through meetings between science and mathematics departments, but others have more serious implications for the construction of curriculum and syllabus.

A small point of complaint is that 3-figure tables are now used in mathematics rather than 4-figure or 6-figure tables. The mathematics teacher usually argues that most scientific calculations in school laboratories involve data which are only correct to two or three figures, and therefore answers are only possible to this accuracy. If this is so, it can be actually misleading to use four figures in such situations. The main reason for the change is, of course that 3-figure tables are easier to use, since 4-figure tables, as normally printed, involve difference columns, whereas 3-figure tables do not. They can therefore be introduced earlier in the course. It is interesting to recall that it was the mathematics teachers of the time who introduced 4-figure tables into the schools when the standard tables in use had seven figures and were printed in substantial books.

* *The Mathematics Curriculum: Mathematics across the Curriculum*, a book in this series, discusses these difficulties in more detail.

It is hoped that science teachers find these reasons acceptable, and are willing to consider carefully the degree of accuracy which they really require. Nowadays it is possible to suggest that, if higher accuracy is needed, an electronic calculator can be brought into use; even so, warning needs to be given that answers cannot be more accurate than the data, and figures should not be recorded just because they are there on the display.

NOTATIONAL PROBLEMS

Several problems of a minor nature arise over the use of common symbols, especially if textbooks or reference books which are non-British are in use. Here again discussion between teachers of different subjects can be fruitful in resolving difficulties, and there is now a standard authority in the shape of the British Standards Institution booklet on *Letter Symbols, Signs and Abbreviations*, or the Royal Society's Report *Quantities, Units and Symbols*, which can be referred to in case of doubt.

Confusion easily arises between the use of a dot (.) for multiplication and the decimal point. Since the decimal point is commonly written as 5,7 or 5.7 outside this country, and increasingly within it, the use of 5.7 to mean 5×7 is certainly to be deprecated. As computer language becomes increasingly familiar, it is even possible that $5*7$ may supersede both.

It is recommended for the same reason that twenty-two thousand three hundred should be written as 22 300 and not as 22,300, which a European will read as 22·300.

What is the meaning of $13 - 2 \times 3$? The old rules say 7, but if the problem is given verbatim to an electronic calculator the answer will be 33. In algebra we can write $a - bc$ without ambiguity, and because of this we should probably agree that $\times$ and $\div$ bind more closely than $+$ and $-$. Further than this we need not go, and all (usually misremembered) mnemonics are best left in oblivion. In all doubtful cases, use brackets. If electronic calculators of a sufficient level of sophistication are available, there is opportunity for some useful lessons in the meaning of brackets and the art of organizing calculations.

Much attention has been paid to three different uses of the minus sign, viz. as part of the symbol for a number, as a binary operation and as an operator "take the additive inverse of". Thus mathematics teachers are pointing out that in these three situations: -3, $4-3$, and $-(+4)$, the minus sign is being used in three different ways. To emphasize this distinction it is usual to say "negative 3" for the number -3. These two usages are seen together, for example, in finding the temperature difference between 4°C and -3°C. We would say "four minus negative three equals four plus three, which is seven". At a time when children are making mistakes in such calculations, it is clearly necessary that the language should be consistent, and a case can be made out for a notational difference also, allocating $^{-}3$ as the symbol for the directed number, at any rate in the early stages.

One of the main complaints from users about modern teaching is that there is not enough emphasis on units of measure in the teaching of number. In a formula such as $t = x/v$, the mathematics teacher is apt to regard x and v as variables on sets of numbers ("pronumerals") and to calculate the value of t as a number from a given pair of numerical replacements for x and y. If the formula has arisen from a practical situation, he will then complete the work with a symbol-free statement: "... $t = 15$. The time taken is 15 seconds." The physicist, however, will want to lay more emphasis throughout on the units of measure involved. He may adopt one of two different methods of doing this.

(a) He may take the mathematician's point of view that t, x, and v stand for *numbers*, but insist that the units are stated in the equation, thus:

$$t(s) = \frac{x(m)}{v(m\,s^{-1})}$$

which implies both the numerical equation $t = x/v$ and the

equation $s = m/(m\,s^{-1})$ involving the units.

(b) Alternatively, he may take the view which is commoner among engineers, that t, x and v stand for *quantities*, which must be given as numbers of units. In this case he will write, for example,

$$x = 50\,m, \quad v = 10\,m\,s^{-1}, \quad \text{so that} \quad t = \frac{x}{v} = \frac{50\,m}{10\,m\,s^{-1}} = 5\,s.$$

(See also *Mathematics across the Curriculum*, chapter 3).

In some ways the second method is preferable, since the equation $t = x/v$ holds universally, no matter what the units are, whereas in (a) $t = x/v$ only if they are the measures in a consistent set of units. Method (b) also seems to correspond more to children's natural tendencies; everyone *says* "area = length times breadth" and writes "$A = l \times b$" to mean this. In the same way we say "the length is 50 metres" and write $l = 50\,m$, where l is the length and m is a metre. This emphasizes that we are really dealing with a *ratio*: $l/m = 50$, and some physicists will actually write this:

$$\frac{t}{s} = \frac{x/m}{v/(m\,s^{-1})} = \frac{50}{10} = 5, \quad \text{so that} \quad t = 5s.$$

Example. To make the point clear, let us find the area of a reel of tape 3 km long and 0·5 cm wide in the two systems.

(a) If the length is l m, the breadth b m, and the area A m², then

$$A(m^2) = l(m) \times b(m) \quad \text{and} \quad A = l \times b.$$

Now $l = 3 \times 10^3$, $b = 0{\cdot}5 \times 10^{-2} = 5 \times 10^{-3}$,

so that $A = 3 \times 10^3 \times 5 \times 10^{-3} = 15$, and the area is $15\,m^2$.

(b) The area $A = l \times b = 3\,km \times 0{\cdot}5\,cm$
$$= 3 \times 10^3\,m \times 0{\cdot}5 \times 10^{-2}\,m$$
$$= 3 \times 10^3 \times 0{\cdot}5 \times 10^{-2}\,m^2$$
$$= 1{\cdot}5 \times 10\,m^2 = 15\,m^2.$$

This is a situation where it is wise to discover which method the various users prefer; fruitful discussion may arise from such an inquiry. Traditionally in mathematics letters have stood for numbers and for nothing else, but modern mathematics has taught us that this need not be so. It could be quite legitimate to say "let p be the price of a peach" or "suppose v is the speed of the train".

The main points to be established are as follows:

(1) *Addition or subtraction* of like quantities can be effected by adding or subtracting their measures in the same unit; £3 + 57p = £3 + £0·57 = £3·57.

(2) The *ratio* of two like quantities can be found by dividing their measures *in the same unit*; it is a pure number. Thus $5 \text{ km} : 200 \text{ m} = 5 \times 10^3 \text{ m} : 2 \times 10^2 \text{ m} = 50 : 2 = 25$. Or, if preferred, $\dfrac{5 \text{ km}}{200 \text{ m}} = \dfrac{5}{200} \dfrac{\text{km}}{\text{m}} = \dfrac{1}{40} \times 1000 = 25$.

(3) Any quantity can, of course, be multiplied or divided by a number: 5 books weighing 0·8 kg each together weigh $5 \times 0·8 \text{ kg} = 4 \text{ kg}$.

(4) Multiplication of lengths produces area and volume; it is convenient to have the units the same, so that $5 \text{ cm} \times 4 \text{ cm} = 20 \text{ cm}^2$ and $2 \text{ m} \times 3 \text{ m} \times 4 \text{ m} = 24 \text{ m}^3$. (The SI symbols for the units have the great advantage that this is now exactly the same as the situation in algebra—another reason for considering such abbreviations as c.c. and sq. ft. as obsolete.)

(5) Multiplication or division of *different* quantities produces a quantity of yet a third kind, which may or may not have useful meaning. Examples which occur in mathematics include

$$3 \text{ men} \times 5 \text{ days} = 15 \text{ man-days}$$
$$60 \text{ km} \div 2 \text{ h} = 30 \text{ km/h}.$$

Here a man-day is a unit of *production* and a km/h is a unit of *velocity*, both of which are quantities of a new kind. As soon as this is done we are involved in the question of *dimensions* which, except in the very simplest cases, is not really a matter for the mathematics department.

Problems of timing have arisen in the introduction of negative indices and in the use of decimals and fractions. This is partly because mathematics teachers have tended to delay the introduction of certain topics until they can hope that they will be properly understood. For example, negative indices are used in the first year of the Nuffield Physics "O" Level course, whereas many mathematics courses defer them until the third year. In this case, physics teachers are probably interested purely in the representation of numbers in scientific notation, whereas mathematics teachers are interested in operating with indices in general. If this is agreed, a compromise can usually be arrived at.

These and many other similar difficulties are dealt with more fully in the companion book: *Mathematics across the Curriculum.*

7 Logarithms and Slide Rules [*]

7.0. Introduction

Since logarithms and slide rules used to hold a prominent place in any "O" Level course, we include a chapter to consider their present role. Owing to the introduction of the electronic calculator, the case for devoting a lot of time to their use has weakened. However, logarithms and slide rules embody an important mathematical idea, which should be encountered by more-able pupils.

In a traditional course, logarithms are usually introduced before slide rules. Neither is expected to be fully understood, and it is hoped that understanding will improve as they are used for computation.

The *SMP* introduces slide rules (*Book C*, p. 132 and *Book 2*, p. 171) taking the view that slide rules are easier to use than logarithms and their 2-figure accuracy will be sufficient for most computation.

The explanation of how the scale was made and why it works (*Book C*, p. 136) is difficult for most children. Logarithms are not used for calculations in the *SMP* course until *Book Z*, chapter 2 and *Book* 4, chapter 4. *MME* takes a more traditional view, and both logarithms and slide rule are introduced in year 2 (*IB*, chapters 18 and 20) where there is a strong arithmetic emphasis.

There are at present many different opinions about the introduction of the slide rule and logarithms. Let us therefore consider exactly what ideas are involved.

7.1. Logarithms

The idea of logarithms develops from the multiplication and division of numbers in standard index form. In a calculation of the type $(1\cdot1 \times 10^2) \times (3\cdot2 \times 10^3)$, we can contrast the way in which the multiplication of the powers of ten is comparatively easy compared with the more laborious calculation $1\cdot1 \times 3\cdot2$. This leads to the suggestion that it might also be possible to write $1\cdot1$ and $3\cdot2$ as powers of ten.

At this point it is much easier to accept the interpolation on the graph $y = 10^x$ than it is to justify it mathematically. If we accept the "continuous" graph $y = 10^x$, it is not difficult to imagine that every positive real number y will be some power (x) of 10.

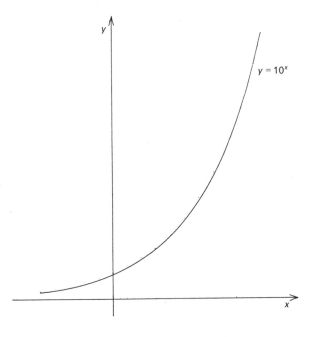

$y = 10^x$

* This chapter is based on an article by T. J. Fletcher.

It is instructive at this stage to place emphasis upon the finding of intermediate values (or numerical interpolation) in calculations such as

(a) $(10^{0.3})^{10} = 10^{0.3} \times 10^{0.3} \times \ldots \times 10^{0.3} = 10^3 = 1000$ but $2^{10} = 1024 \simeq 1000$. Hence $2 \simeq 10^{0.3}$.

From this we get at once that $4 \simeq 10^{0.6}$, $8 \simeq 10^{0.9}$, $5 \simeq 10^{0.7}$. Since $3^4 = 81 \simeq 80 \simeq 10^{1.9}$, we have $3 \simeq 10^{0.48}$ and $6 \simeq 10^{0.78}$. Finally $7^2 = 49 \simeq 50 \simeq 10^{1.7}$ leads to $7 \simeq 10^{0.85}$, and the logarithms of all integers from 1 to 9 are estimated to two places. The only one, in fact, which is not correct to two places is $\log 9$ $(= 0.95424\ldots)$ which is given by this method as 0.96.

(b) We can find approximations for $\log_2 3$ by an iterative procedure as follows: we know that $\log_2 2 = 1$ and $\log_2 4 = 2$; hence $\log_2 \sqrt{2 \times 4} = \log_2 2.828 = 1.5$. As $2.828 < 3 < 4$, $\log_2 2.828 < \log_2 3 < \log_2 4$, i.e. $1.5 < \log_2 3 < 2$. Repeating the process, $\log_2 \sqrt{2.828 \times 4} = 1.75$ and thus $1.5 < \log_2 3 < 1.75$.

This is a poor method of calculation, but it helps us to understand the interpolation in the continuous graph.

7.2. Slide Rules

There are several different ideas needed to understand the slide rule, and we must not be tempted to present them all at once. First we should consider how two rulers can be used as a machine for addition and subtraction. Since the rulers have the same scale, by *comparing* the readings at one point, we compare readings at another point:

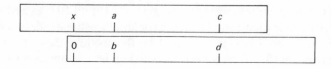

Thus $c - d = a - b$.

By looking at two rulers in this way, we can see a relationship between two sets of numbers.

By checking the number x against the zero, we have $x + d = c$, the addition step for the rulers which is analogous to the multiplication step for the slide rule.

As a second preliminary activity, we should look at a logarithmic scale, sometimes called a Gunter scale, which was invented in 1623, soon after Napier published his work on logarithms (1594–1614). In all work using a *logarithmic scale*, the essential idea is that equal displacements correspond to equal multiplications. This is an idea that needs time to be assimilated.

We might look at a situation such as the old story about the grains of rice on the squares of a chessboard, in which the number of grains is multiplied by a constant (in this case 2) for each further square. If we mark the number of grains on a logarithmic scale, then the marks are equidistant as they represent equal multipliers. The time scale in 6.1 is another logarithmic scale.

Examples of naturally occurring geometrical progressions which can be marked in this way are:

(1) Camera stops, associated with the numbers

2, 2·8, 4, 5·6, 8, 11, 16, 22, 32.

(2) Standard paper sizes, using the series of numbers

1189	841	594	420	297	210	148 etc.
A0	A1	A2	A3	A4	A5	

Thus A4 paper measures 297 mm by 210 mm.

In a further development, we might use logarithmic graph paper (i.e. with one logarithmic scale) to get a straight-line relationship in the examples above.

7.3. The Relationship between Logarithms and Slide Rules

The isomorphism between

$$1 \quad 2 \quad 4 \quad 8 \quad 16 \quad 32 \quad \dots \quad \text{with} \times$$
$$0 \quad 1 \quad 2 \quad 3 \quad 4 \quad 5 \quad \dots \quad \text{with} +$$

is discussed in many modern texts, such as
Midland Mathematics Experiment: *IA*, ch. 8; *IB*, ch. 18. (Harrap),
SMP: *Book C*, ch. 9; *Book E*, ch. 8; *Book G*, ch. 2. (CUP),
MMS: *Book 4*, Arithmetic ch. 1 (Blackie/Chambers).

Historically speaking this first appeared in the form

$$\dots \quad -3 \quad -2 \quad -1 \quad 0 \quad 1 \quad 2 \quad 3 \quad \dots$$
$$\dots \quad \quad 8 \quad \quad 4 \quad \quad 2 \quad 0 \quad \tfrac{1}{2} \quad \tfrac{1}{4} \quad \tfrac{1}{8} \quad \dots$$

(Stifel, *Arithmetica Integra*, 1524.)

It is interesting to compare how the various books proceed from the isomorphism to the slide rule. The isomorphism may be indicated by

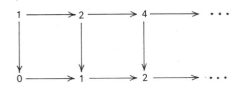

The essential idea is that two numbers in the upper row may be multiplied by adding the corresponding numbers in the lower row.

Looking at this arrow diagram, we can regard the bottom row as the scale for the pair of rulers, and the top row as the scale for the slide rules. Thus as the rulers gave us a machine for addition and subtraction, so the slide rule gives a machine for multiplication and division.

The isomorphism is also a line of approach to the understanding of logarithms. The number in the lower row is called the *logarithm* (or *index*) of the number in the upper row. Of course, at the moment we are talking of *logarithms to base* 2. We may draw the diagram

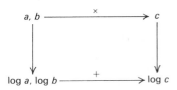

In this diagram the vertical arrow denotes the operation of taking the logarithm; or in other words it denotes the function

$$f: x \mapsto \log x$$

or

$$x \mapsto y \quad \text{where } x = 2^y$$

We can only find logarithms of numbers which happen to be powers of 2, and so we need to look for the logarithms of other numbers as in the calculations above. A refinement is to take some other number as the base of logarithms; say 1·1. This enables many points to be plotted on the associated graph. The business of taking powers of 1·1 is a simple matter on an electronic calculator.

Tables of greater accuracy may be calculated by taking numbers still closer to 1 as the base. (Napier's first tables of log sines used as base 0·9999999 and the calculations involved, using the methods of his time, were phenomenal.)

This means that it is possible to standardize logarithms by choosing the particular number that is to have logarithm unity, whatever base has been used for the calculations in the first place, and in practice it is convenient to arrange for log 10 to be unity.

As an exercise we might take powers of 1·1 until 10 is exceeded and, by making judicious linear interpolations, estimate the logs of 2, 3, 5, 7 and 10 (logs to base 1·1). By dividing these by the logarithm of 10, we can convert these to logs base 10 and check the answers with tables. (Surprising accuracy is obtainable by this method.)

It should not be necessary here to go into the details of *characteristic* and *mantissa*, and the practical use of three or four-figure tables. The teacher who wishes to do this will notice one or two small gaps in the above outline, which require filling in. The use of logarithm tables is hardly to be encouraged as a regular method of doing the multiplications and divisions which are needed in scientific calculation, but in some circumstances teachers may still need to teach this.

It would seem reasonable to discuss the use of logarithms for such tasks as the extraction of roots, because these are applications of the central idea; but if pupils have any difficulties with such things as negative characteristics, rather than drilling them on this it would be better to devote the time to more profitable mathematics.

However, the logarithmic relation remains a most important idea, and it should certainly receive careful and extensive treatment in any "O" Level course, while logarithms do not so obviously belong to a CSE course.

There are severe drawbacks to defining a logarithm as an index, and these will certainly have to be tackled in the sixth form if they are not tackled before. We cannot discuss this here, but an alternative approach is to define a logarithm by means of the area under the curve $y = 1/x$, and it is quite possible to do this as part of an "O" Level course.

The considerations of this section lead us back to the logarithmic scale. We must repeat that if we accept on experimental evidence that it is possible to construct a number-line along which equal displacements correspond to equal multiplications, then we have all the foundation that we need for the practical use of the slide rule. The use of various forms of slide rule (without any theory) as a tables-remembrancer for less-able pupils should be considered (see the Kesty slide rule described in chapter 8, p. 77).

7.4. The Slide Rule as a Proportionalizer

Since equal steps along a Gunter scale correspond to equal multiplications, a pair of side-by-side scales will work as a proportionalizer. Doing individual calculations by individual settings of the slide rule is a more complicated idea which should come later. At the present stage we need to see just how much can be obtained from one setting of the slide rule only. When teaching children, for long periods of the lesson we will set the slide rule to one position, leave it there, and learn all we can.

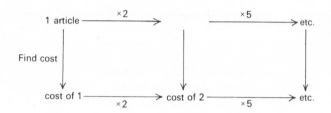

What *is* a proportion? We could do far worse than to say

a proportion is a setting of the slide rule.

When we consider a particular proportion, the arrow diagram above is "immersed" in the slide rule, and the pairs of numbers in proportion are displayed side by side.

The slide rule is a proportionalizer.

Much experimental work can be done on this using strips of logarithmic graph paper, with the pupils marking the numbers they want, or labelling the scales according to the particular uses to which they are being put.

As an exercise some special-purpose slide rules might be designed. The base-2 slide rule seems a rather naive instrument, but it has applications in photography (see below). Some pupils might like to adapt a base-2 slide rule (drawn on *ordinary* graph paper) to a time-for-a-journey calculator. The speed is to be pre-set, perhaps using little pictures of people walking, running, etc., and the distances and corresponding times are to be displayed side by side

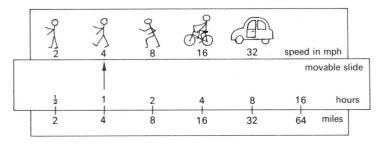

When the principles have been understood, slide rules may be constructed for a variety of other applications. These permit a wide range of pupils to participate in related activity. Those who find mathematics easy may design calculating devices themselves, others may use such devices to perform (or to check) routine calculations, even if they do not understand all of the theory

involved. (Of course, we never give up hope; we hope that through use the theory may become better understood as time goes on, and we design our teaching around this hope.)

As another exercise we might investigate the exposure meter which is given by Kodak as part of their excellently documented CSE course, *Fundamentals of Photography*

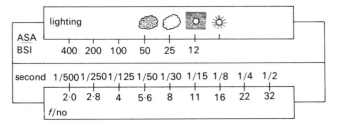

In this chapter, we have drawn attention to the mathematical importance of logarithms and slide rules, and we have suggested some possible work which draws attention to the applications. As an aid to computation, logarithm tables are often outdated, but they should not therefore be excluded from the curriculum.

8 Aids and Apparatus

8.0. Introduction

Apparatus can be used in various ways. It can be used by the teacher for demonstration; it can be designed by the pupils or operated by them; it can be commercially produced, or made by teacher or class. Some apparatus will be used as an aid to the understanding of basic concepts; the greater hand the pupil has in making it, the more benefit he is likely to derive from its use. Apparatus of this kind we describe in the first section. Many teachers will already have their own favourite aids, and we hope that our comments will enable them to view these more critically. In the later sections we discuss the use of various aids to computation which cannot be made in the classroom—though the principles on which they work can sometimes be shown by home-made models.

8.1. Aids to Demonstrate Basic Concepts

(a) THE INTEGERS

Every secondary classroom where mathematics is taught might well contain a visual wall chart of the positive number-line, say to 100, divided evenly into 100 parts. In the first-year secondary stage this would probably be a single line, thickly drawn on a continuous strip, each number being indicated, with the multiples of 10 displayed more boldly.

The next stage might be to mark the numbers of special significance in some way (e.g. drawing a □ under square numbers and a ⌷ under cubes).

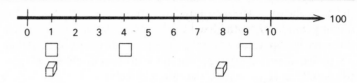

Then the negative section of the line should be added (perhaps in another colour?).

Sometimes the emphasis upon different sets makes numbers harder for the average pupil. The integer line is a clear and simple model for integers. It can obviously be used for linear measurement, but other situations like bank balances can also be modelled on the integer line.

It is clearly shown on the model that some integers are whole numbers, and some whole numbers are squares. Constant use of the integers in this geometric situation prepares the way for questions about measurement with rational numbers and real numbers.

By geometry, it is seen that negative 10 is a reflection of positive 10 with the mirror at 0, and that the numbers on the negative side are equally spaced, like those on the positive side. If < is defined as meaning "to the left of", then it will be seen that just as $15 > 10$, so $-15 < -10$, and so on.

(b) PLACE VALUE

(i) *Multiplication and division by 10 with a sliding card*

In this piece of apparatus illustrated on p. 74, multiplication by 10 can be shown on the front and division by 10 on the back. All that is needed is two pieces of fairly stiff card, say 10 in by 8 in, with triangular pieces of card separating them, so that another card can slide diagonally between them. The cards have windows cut in them, as shown; the zeros, however, are permanently marked in dummy windows on the fixed cards. Other digits can be written through the top windows on the sliding card (front or back); when it is pulled down the digits appear in the bottom windows, and give the number × 10 or ÷ 10 as the case may be.

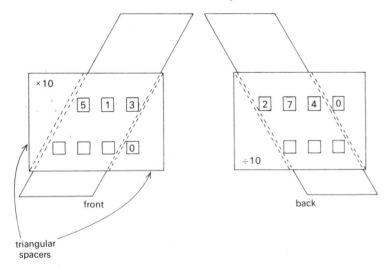

front   back

triangular
spacers

(ii) *Powers of ten slide-rule*

This apparatus needs a little more careful construction, but is mathematically a good deal more versatile. It is probably best to have the digits permanently marked on it.

ⓐ and ⓑ are fixed. ⓒ slides along carrying the digits with it, together with a window ⓓ which reveals the change in *value* of ⓑ, e.g. × 10 or ÷ 10. Note that the decimal point remains fixed and the place values are moved.

We should make certain that such aids actually help with the

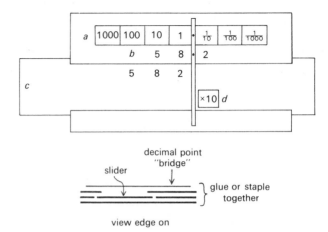

decimal point
"bridge"
slider
} glue or staple
together

view edge on

child's difficulty. In (i), we assume that he recognizes 513 and 5130 but he is unable to relate them together. It may be he does not immediately connect 5 − 1 − 3 − 0 in the windows with 5130. In (ii), he may not understand the meaning of the numbers 1000, 100,...etc. along the top line and this is the first step in using the aid.

(c) SUBTRACTION

Subtraction may be recognized as the "measure" of the gap between any two numbers on the number-line, e.g.

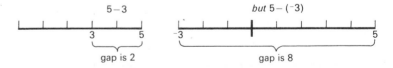

5 − 3   *but* 5 − (⁻3)

gap is 2   gap is 8

The model shown below is a demonstration model and is not flexible enough for more than 2 examples. It can be made simply from card fastened with tape or, more solidly, from wood joined with a hinge. The hinge indicates zero on the number-line. We fold the two pieces together for subtraction of two positive numbers, or open them out for the subtraction of a negative from a positive number, e.g.

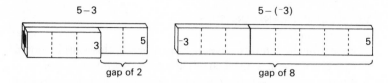

The sign for the answer is given by the *direction* of the gap, i.e. for $+5-(+2)$, we want the gap *from* $+2$ *to* $+5$ and this gap is positive.

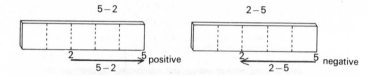

We recognize subtraction in three different situations: to *take away*, to *make up* and to find *the difference*, and this aid is based upon the third of these situations, finding the difference or the gap between numbers.

(d) FRACTIONS

(i) For comparing sizes and equivalent fractions, a card consisting of separate marked cards showing various parts making one whole unit is a long-established visual aid (see top of next column).

A modification (suggested in *Mathematics Teaching*, March 1975, "Two Approaches to Equivalence of Fractions" by P. G. Scopes) is the following. It develops the concept of the number-line, which requires concepts of *equal lengths* and the idea of *labelling points* to mark the end of successive equal intervals.

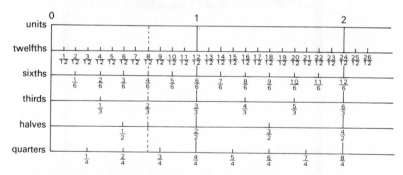

We draw a number of different number-lines with different-sized fractional intervals (without "cancellation"), starting with (say) the twelfths. We stress that successive intervals along the line are marked by points whose labels have increasing numerators, but whose denominators remain constant, giving the scale a *name*, in the first case the twelfths scale. Underneath this we can now write a variety of other scales, drawn in such a way that the various representations of full units are clearly equivalent in view of the fact that they are vertically below one another.

The representations of equivalent fractions can now be seen *with their corresponding labels* by simply viewing corresponding lengths on the various scales. For example, it is clear that $\frac{2}{3}$, $\frac{4}{6}$, $\frac{8}{12}$ each represent points the same distance along the number-line, but are different ways of referring to it.

(ii) This now familiar picture from *SMP* is used to demonstrate equivalent fractions or to arrange fractions in size order. It will be much more effective if the diagonal marker is a movable rod, pivoted at 0, rather than drawn on the paper.

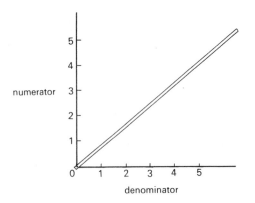

The article referred to above ("Two Approaches to Equivalence of Fractions" by P. G. Scopes) has further suggestions developed from this picture.

(e) MULTIPLES AND DIVISORS

(i) *Factor sieve*

Based on the famous sieve of Eratosthenes, this simple model consists of 100 cubes, marked as shown and set into a frame.

On the reverse side, the cubes are held in place with (approx.) 3 mm-thick elastic. Pupils can be invited to push out all multiples of 2, 3, etc., to discover primes to 100, or to discover divisor combinations for a given number.

1	2	3	4	5	6	7	8	9	10
11	12	13	14	15	16	17	18	19	20
21	22	23	24	25	26	27	28	29	30
31	32	33	34	35	36	37	38	39	40
41	42	43	44	45	46	47	48	49	50
51	52	53	54	55	56	57	58	59	60
61	62	63	64	65	66	67	68	69	70
71	72	73	74	75	76	77	78	79	80
81	82	83	84	85	86	87	88	89	90
91	92	93	94	95	96	97	98	99	100

on reverse

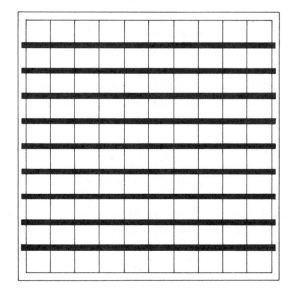

(ii) *Divisors chart*

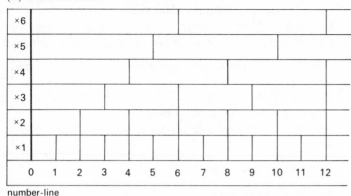

number-line

The "stops" above an integer on the number-line represent the positive divisors of that number, and so the primes may be identified by the fact that they have exactly two stops above them. Reading across a horizontal line, the stops represent the multiples of the number chosen. At a more sophisticated level one may use the chart to find LCMs and HCFs. Picking two numbers on the vertical axis, their LCM is the first number at which both numbers stop. Using the horizontal axis, a similar procedure gives the HCF of two numbers, and both techniques extend to LCMs and HCFs of more than two numbers.

If the chart is drawn with more tracks, say up to 16, the square numbers may be seen as those having an odd number of stops. (A coloured version should be made to see its effectiveness.)

(iii) *A simple slide rule*

Illustrated above (on the right) is the Kesty slide rule. This postcard-length ruler gives multiples up to 81. If the moving section is inverted, factors are given for any chosen multiple.

(Any correspondence regarding the Kesty should be addressed to its inventor, Mr. J. Beaney, 9 Stonelea, The Quarry, Dursley, Glos.)

moving slide

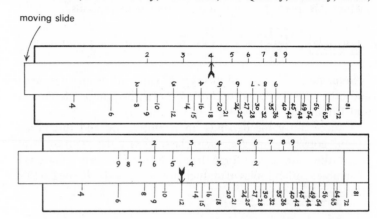

At the simplest level the ruler gives ready and easy access to products and divisors in an interesting slide-rule form which is found to be far more stimulating than the static traditional table.

At a deeper level, use of the ruler has led to an early and successful introduction of more sophisticated slide rules and an appreciation of logarithms at a surprisingly early age.

(f) DOMINO GAMES

(i) Practice in four rules. "Dominoes" provide a pleasant way to revise the four rules, by arranging a set of cards, beginning and ending with an asterisk. Unused cards indicate errors. It is easy to prepare a set of twelve 5 cm × 10 cm cards by cutting up a 20 cm × 30 cm sheet; the cards are then shuffled and the child arranges them like dominoes. It is important that no two answers are the same. The teacher can make a set to suit the needs of individual children (see below).

| ∗ | 2+4 | | 6 | 3+7 | | 10 | 4+7 | | 11 | 3+9 | | 12 | 5+3 |

| 8 | 6+9 | | 15 | 2+11 | | 13 | 6÷3 +5 | | 14 | 7+9 | | 16 | ∗ |

(ii) Dominoes may be designed for other situations, for example, to show fractions in various forms: vulgar, decimal, picture. The players match, in turn, equivalent fractions.

    and so on.

Some more examples of this type of game are given on page 41 and others can be found in *Starting Points* by Banwell, Saunders and Tahta.

A successful game depends upon motivation and this needs careful consideration for each class. Given the right sort of motivation, such games force the pupils to revise their knowledge of numbers; other topics in mathematics can also be learned in this way.

8.2. Mechanical Calculators

Recent technological advances have had a considerable influence on the types of calculating devices at present available. In terms of speed and compactness, the electronic varieties win hands down over their old-fashioned mechanical counterparts; of this there can be no question. What is sometimes disputed is their relative value as *teaching* devices compared with other calculating aids. We give two specific examples to illustrate this point.

The hand calculator has great value in secondary school in giving an understanding of the place value notation. It also helps with the idea of multiplication as repeated addition, and division as repeated subtraction.

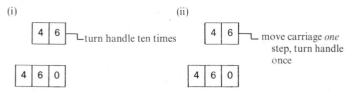

Some practice in using the second method to multiply by ten will reinforce the understanding of place value.

An allied problem concerns the characteristic of a logarithm, and again the hand calculator proves to be a useful teaching aid.

First. Place a single digit in the units column of the calculator.   e.g. [2]

Then wind the handle 4 times.   [8]

Clear the machine, or use another machine.

Place the same single digit in the units column of the calculator.   [2]

Then move the *carriage* one place.   [2][0]

Then wind the handle 4 times.   [8][0]

Repeat, moving the carriage successively 2, 3, 4, 5,... times. Emphasize that the movement of the carriage by one step is equivalent to increasing the characteristic of the logarithm of the number produced in it by ONE. Thus the following table may be formed:

Number having ONE digit value (1–9·9). Characteristic is 0
Number having TWO digit value (10–99). Characteristic is 1
Number having THREE digit value (100–999). Characteristic is 2
and so on.

8.3. Using Electronic Calculators

It is difficult to describe the effective use of electronic calculators because, like pencils and paper, they should be available for use when required, rather than taught for their own sake.

The following lesson suddenly became more vivid because a calculator was at hand, although it was not the original intention to "use calculators". (This lesson is also described in an article by D. S. Hale in *Mathematics Teaching* 67, June 1974.)

A fifth-year class was working on the problem of making open boxes by cutting equal corners from a square sheet of metal (the diagram at the top of p. 79 illustrates the process).
One group had taken a 15-cm square and was calculating the volumes which result when corners of different sizes are removed.

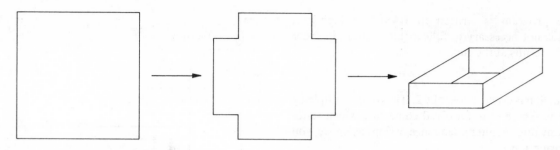

Size of corner removed (cm)	Dimensions of box (cm)	Volume (cm³)
1	$13 \times 13 \times 1$	169
2	$11 \times 11 \times 2$	242
3	$9 \times 9 \times 3$	243
4	$7 \times 7 \times 4$	196
5	$5 \times 5 \times 5$	125
6	$3 \times 3 \times 6$	54
7	$1 \times 1 \times 7$	7

The question: Which corner size produces a maximum volume? arose spontaneously, and after some discussion some points were plotted on a graph.

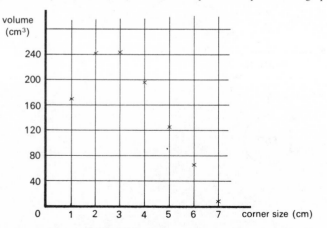

But what happens between 2 cm and 3 cm? The disagreement about this was amiable but vigorous. Some said that 243 cm³ was the maximum volume, others said that you could do better by taking a corner size somewhere between 2 cm and 3 cm. Majority opinion favoured a value nearer to 3 cm than to 2 cm: a very plausible interpretation of the isolated points they had plotted.

Someone then suggested that they should try 2·5 cm and, without much difficulty, they arrived at

$$10 \times 10 \times 2 \cdot 5 = 250.$$

Well, 250 was the best value achieved so far, but the general feeling was that we could do even better. At this stage they made use of Michael's pocket electronic calculator which he happened, by good fortune, to have brought to that particular lesson. Some of the resulting computation is given below.

$$9 \cdot 8 \ \times \ 9 \cdot 8 \ \times 2 \cdot 6 \ = 249 \cdot 704$$
$$9 \cdot 6 \ \times \ 9 \cdot 6 \ \times 2 \cdot 7 \ = 248 \cdot 832$$
$$9 \cdot 9 \ \times \ 9 \cdot 9 \ \times 2 \cdot 55 = 249 \cdot 9255$$
$$9 \cdot 98 \times \ 9 \cdot 98 \times 2 \cdot 51 = 249 \cdot 997004$$
$$10 \cdot 2 \ \times 10 \cdot 2 \ \times 2 \cdot 4 \ = 249 \cdot 696$$
$$10 \cdot 1 \ \times 10 \cdot 1 \ \times 2 \cdot 45 = 249 \cdot 9245$$

By the end of the lesson everyone seemed convinced that 250 cm³ was the maximum volume.

8.4. Using a Computer Terminal

INVESTIGATION I. A PROBLEM IN NUMBER THEORY

The unsolved problem in number theory described on page 45, number IV, was investigated using a computer terminal. It was possible to get a lot of information very rapidly, and by using the on-line terminal the instructions could be changed as the problem developed. The program is written in BASIC, a high-level language, but it is not necessary to follow the program in order to understand the results at the end.

The problem

Take an integer. If it is even, divide it by 2. If it is odd, multiply by three and add one. There is an unsolved conjecture which states that if you take any integer, after a sequence of steps as above, you will eventually reach 1, e.g.

$$20 \underset{\div 2}{\to} 10 \underset{\div 2}{\to} 5 \underset{\times 3+1}{\longrightarrow} 16 \underset{\div 2}{\to} 8 \underset{\div 2}{\to} 4 \underset{\div 2}{\to} 2 \underset{\div 2}{\to} 1$$

$$3 \to 10 \to 5 \to 16 \to 8 \to 4 \to 2 \to 1.$$

The program

The program asks for an input X, the integer to be tested and prints N, the number of steps taken to reach 1.

At each step, X is replaced either by $Y = X/2$ or $Z = 3X + 1$. The first decision (50) is whether the work should stop, i.e. have we reached 1? The second decision (60) is whether X should be replaced by Y or Z, i.e. is X even or odd?

Each instruction is numbered so that the instructions are obeyed in sequential order. However, they may be "typed" in any order so that modifications can be made at any stage.

```
10   INPUT X
20   N = 0
30   N = N + 1
40   Y = X/2
50   IF  Y = 1 THEN  70
60   If  Y > INT (Y) THEN  65
61   X = Y
62   GOTO 30
65   Z = 3*X + 1
66   X = Z
67   GOTO 30
70   PRINT N
90   END
```

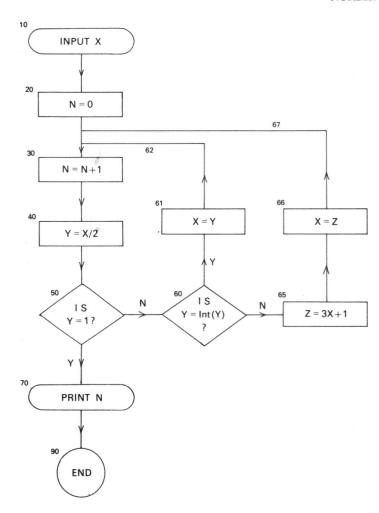

Results

The following tests were made:

INPUT 20	PRINT OUT 7
INPUT 27	PRINT OUT 111

This shows that it takes 7 steps and 111 steps for the numbers 20 and 27 respectively, viz.

$$20 \to 10 \to 5 \to 16 \to 8 \to 4 \to 2 \to 1$$

Program Modification

```
10  INPUT A, B
11  X = A
70  If N < 50  THEN 81
80  PRINT A, N
81  A = A + 1
82  IF A < (B+1) THEN 11
```

In the modification, the computer will now test all the integers between A and B (inclusive) and print the integer together with the number of steps if the number of steps is 50 or more.

Further results

The following test was made:

INPUT 2, 40	
PRINT OUT	27 111
	31 106

This shows that it takes more than fifty steps in only two cases among the integers 2–40. 27 and 31 both belong to the sequence

$$27 \to 82 \to 41 \to 124 \to 62 \to 31 \to \ldots$$

and so 27 takes 5 more steps than 31.

Although it is possible to build up information about this conjecture, if it is true, it cannot be proved true by using the computer. If it is false, it might be possible to find a counter-example by using a computer.

INVESTIGATION II. PYTHAGORAS *v.* NEWTON

In these three lessons, the methods of Pythagoras and Newton to get an approximation to $\sqrt{2}$ were compared, and the outcome would have been virtually impossible without the availability of a computer.

Lesson 1

No machines were available and long division was used.

Problem

Pythagoras had a method for getting rational approximations to $\sqrt{2}$. He knew that if a/b is an approximation for $\sqrt{2}$ then $(a+2b)/(a+b)$ is a better one. Obtain a series of approximations, starting with $a/b = 1/1 = x_1$.

Solution

a	b	$a+2b$	$a+b$	$(a+2b)/(a+b) \simeq \sqrt{2}$	
1	1	3	2	1·5	x_2
3	2	7	5	1·4	x_3
7	5	17	12	1·4167	x_4
17	12	41	29	1·4138	x_5
41	29	99	70	1·4143	x_6

$\sqrt{2} = 1·414$ to 4 significant figures

The pupils were able to see how the rational approximations to $\sqrt{2}$ get closer and closer, being too large and too small alternately. Since the last two values agree to 4 figures, there is little doubt that the result is true to 4 significant figures. Other numbers could be used instead of 2 and they could approximate to $\sqrt{n}$, where $\sqrt{n}$ is irrational, by using $(a+nb)/(a+b)$. It is best to take the first approximation as the nearest whole number to $\sqrt{n}$.

Lesson 2

A hand calculating machine was available. An electronic calculating machine would have been even more useful.

Problem

Newton's method gives a series of approximations for $\sqrt{2}$ thus. If x is an approximation to $\sqrt{2}$, then $\frac{1}{2}(x+2/x)$ is a better one. Is Newton's method superior to Pythagoras' method?

Solution

As above Pythagoras' method gives

$$1 \to \tfrac{3}{2} \to \tfrac{7}{5} \to \tfrac{17}{12} \to \tfrac{41}{29} \to \tfrac{99}{70} \to \ldots$$

i.e. $\qquad 1 \to 1{\cdot}5 \to 1{\cdot}4 \to 1{\cdot}4167 \to 1{\cdot}4138 \to 1{\cdot}4143$.

By Newton's method:

x	$2/x$	$\frac{1}{2}(x+2/x)$
1	2	$\frac{3}{2} = 1{\cdot}5$
$\frac{3}{2}$	$\frac{4}{3}$	$\frac{17}{12} = 1{\cdot}4167$
$\frac{17}{12}$	$\frac{24}{17}$	$\frac{577}{408} = 1{\cdot}41422$

i.e. $\qquad 1 \to 1{\cdot}5 \to 1{\cdot}4167 \to 1{\cdot}41422 \to \ldots$

Newton's method is superior.

Lesson 3

A computer was available to the pupils; by looking at the computer printout, a pupil was able to make a conjecture about the relationship between Newton's method and Pythagoras' method. He conjectured that Newton's method will give the approximations $x_1, x_2, x_4, x_8, x_{16}, \ldots$, where the suffices are powers of 2. (This conjecture can be proved by considering powers of the matrix $A = \begin{pmatrix} 1 & 2 \\ 1 & 1 \end{pmatrix}$. The Pythagorean approximations are related to Ax, A^2x, A^3x, etc., where $x = \begin{pmatrix} 1 \\ 0 \end{pmatrix}$ and the Newtonian approximations are related to Ax, A^2x, A^4x, etc.)

The presence of a machine represents an opportunity to do more enjoyable mathematics rather than just an opportunity to perform quicker and more accurate calculations.

8.5. Electronic Calculators

THE PRESENT SITUATION

The arrival of the electronic pocket calculator in a highly competitive market over the last few years has meant that simple models are now selling at prices which bring them within the reach of a huge proportion of the population. The steady reduction in price has been in marked contrast to general inflation, but seems now to be levelling out. Nevertheless any statements about prices are likely to become quickly out of date.

Many of our pupils now have their own pocket calculators, and many more have access to models owned by their parents or friends. The social impact of this is very great, and such traditional aids to computation as logarithm tables and the slide rule are being rapidly rendered obsolete, at least for most everyday purposes. The old mechanical desk calculator has been completely displaced by its cheaper, more rapid and more versatile rival. Such may still find a use for educational purposes, as we have seen, but their day is done.

USE IN SCHOOL

There are of course dangers in the unrestricted use of pocket calculators, even if it were possible for every child to have his personal model. Employers fear a further decline in ability to perform simple mental calculations, and point out that in real life many such calculations are still required where there is neither time nor facility to refer even to a pocket model—much work still dirties the hands!

There is also the problem of the use of electronic calculators in examinations, where it may be required to test elementary computational processes; also justice may be thought to demand parity of equipment between candidates—compare the issue of standard sets of tables.

It is necessary to offset against these arguments the real advantages of having additional computational power available in the classroom (see section 8.3). Also since the electronic calculator is a tool which everybody is likely to meet in adult life, it could be regarded as a necessary part of education to make children familiar with its potentialities and limitations, and to enable them to assess critically the different types of model and the results that are obtained from them. As with all the gadgets of technology: camera, radio, tape-recorders,…, the mind, judgment, and personal responsibility of the user is more important than mere technical proficiency in its use, just as this in its turn is more valuable than blind reliance on the pronouncements of a supposed expert.

The SMP Computing Group has set up an experiment in six schools across the educational spectrum to assess the usefulness of electronic calculators. Many of the observations which follow are derived from these progress reports, for which due acknowledgement is made. Those who are interested might like to contact Nigel Webb at Oakham School who is acting as a clearing-house for information.

USE IN EXAMINATIONS

The regulations of the various examination boards vary from unrestricted permission in Scotland (except for "O" Grade Arithmetic, Paper 1) to complete exclusion from mathematics examinations. The use of calculators is often allowed in subjects other than mathematics—including commercial mathematics—even when it is forbidden in mathematics itself. They are more usually permitted at "A" Level.

It is desirable that there should be general agreement among the various boards. There seems nothing to lose in allowing free use of an approved model of calculator for all examinations at "A" Level and for all except mathematics examinations at "O" Level. Even here the ban could be confined to one paper, and in this, certain results could be allowed to be left in a form suitable for entry to a calculator, together with a rough estimate of the answer. Consideration needs to be given to the design and use of a standard model for "O" Level or CSE examination purposes, and also to an oral examination in the use of aids to calculation in general; the slide rule also might be included in this if it was felt to be still a valuable educational aid, e.g. for scale changes, conversions and proportions.

WHAT MODEL TO BUY?

We cannot hope to do a *"Which?"* article on electronic calculators, but some guidelines can usefully be given. To begin with, the *New Scientist* published a review article in 1975 (Vol. 65, p. 506) which can be consulted. Up-to-date information can be obtained from Taylor-Wilson Systems Ltd., Oakfield House, Station Road, Dorridge, Solihull B93 8HQ.

Broadly speaking there are three classes of calculator available:

(*a*) *Arithmetic*, giving $+ - \times \div$, preferably with automatic squaring and $\sqrt{\ }$.

(*b*) *Scientific*, giving in addition a store or two, trigonometric functions, log, exp, and their inverses; possibly also mean and standard deviation.

(*c*) *Programmable*, with a store for about 100 program steps entered on the keyboard, the higher-priced models having magnetic-card storage and reading facilities for programs.

For basic school use, type (*a*) is probably sufficient, but it is helpful to have a machine that has a change-sign $(+/-)$ key and deals properly with negative numbers; a store into which addition and subtraction can be effected is more useful than trigonometric functions.

There is a case for equipping every mathematics classroom with a machine of type (*b*) so that more-sophisticated calculations can be carried out when needed.

Questions that need to be asked about any proposed model should include the following:

1 Is it robust enough for the classroom? (What happens if it is dropped?)

2 Does it run on rechargeable batteries? (If not, replacement of batteries may be expensive.)

3 Is it reliable? Are service facilities available and is there a guarantee for replacement of faulty instruments? (Some cheap models have a bad reputation for failure.)

4 Is the keyboard big enough and the keys robust enough for children to use?

5 Is the display large enough to be easily seen and by more than one user? (Especially if it is intended to issue one calculator to two or more pupils. The green displays are discharge-tubes which are usually clearer than the red LED displays, but they are liable to fade with age and they are more fragile.)

6 Does it use algebraic logic? (Reverse Polish is difficult for school use.)

7 Does it express numbers in scientific notation when required? (Usually this means a more expensive machine.)

8 How accurate is it? (Some calculators work to more digits than they display, which is an advantage. Many giving trigonometric functions do not perform very well for angles near 0 and 90° due to slow convergence and rounding errors. A standard test is to enter (in degree mode) 29 : sin : cos : tan :

$e^x : \sqrt{}$: sq : ln : arctan : arcos : arcsin. This is a stringent test since rounding errors can occur (in an 8-place display in the fourth significant figure.)

9 What about security? "Pocket" machines can easily be pocketed! Some models can be locked in security cradles, but this whole question has to be considered in relation to the circumstances prevailing where the machines are to be used.

10 How much does it cost? As in the case of many appliances, here also you get what you pay for. It is first necessary to decide what you really need to have in regular use. If a great deal of sophisticated work of a non-routine type (e.g. not merely straightforward calculation of means and standard deviations) is expected, then it is probably best to investigate the possibility of linkup with a full-scale computer, or a share in a desk-top computer using BASIC, such as the Hewlett-Packard 9800 series.

To sum up, here is a list of operations available in the order of increasing complexity favoured by many manufacturers. Each step up costs money!

$$a \begin{bmatrix} +, \, -, \, \times, \, \div, \, 8 \text{ digit, } (\%) \\ M \text{ (constant only)} \end{bmatrix}$$

$M+, M-, M\times, M\div, Sq, \sqrt{}, (1/x, +/-)$

Recommended level for general use → Rechargeable batteries

Scientific notation: $8+2$ digits, sin, cos, tan, exp, and inverses, π, deg/rad

Recommended specialized level b → Two memories, polar/rectangular conversion, x^y, $\bar{x}$, σ, ( )

Three memories, $10+2$ digits, regression, $x!$, standard conversions

$$c \begin{bmatrix} \text{Keyboard programmable} \\ \text{Magnetic-card programmable, printer} \end{bmatrix}$$

Access available → BASIC typewriter input and output.

9 A More Formal Basis for the Number Systems

9.0. Introduction

The point of view of this chapter may be summarized in the saying of Kronecker: "God made the whole numbers; all else is the work of man". Kronecker was in fact saying that the properties of the rationals, reals, and indeed the whole of analysis ought to be deduced by finite processes from the laws for the whole numbers, and refused to admit what could not be so deduced. Other mathematicians in the nineteenth century used infinite processes in developing analysis from the laws for the whole numbers, and Russell and Whitehead attempted to deduce the laws for whole numbers from the laws of logic.

What are the implications for 11–16 mathematics? It is a common fallacy that it is pedagogically desirable or even possible to introduce the integers, the rationals and the reals in an axiomatic way. Pupils are bound to learn first of all about numbers by example, and only at a later stage as abstract entities.

For example, we saw in chapter 5 that pupils are likely to meet integers as *points* on a scale and as *shifts*. In these contexts, it is natural to talk about their order, addition and subtraction, but multiplication and division do not arise. Much later on, they meet integers as *transformations* of the real number-line and in this context there is a natural multiplication. However. somewhere between these two examples the question arises: "What is -2×-3?", probably motivated by considerations of algebra, or simply by a feeling of incompleteness until it is answered.

This question needs to be answered in different ways according to the context and the pupils' level of understanding. Some possibilities have been suggested in chapter 5. However, later on, probably in the sixth form, pupils will want to face such questions as: "What are the integers?" and "Why do they obey the same laws as the whole numbers?". This chapter is mainly about this formal stage, but teachers of arithmetic at all levels should be aware of the way in which the later stages can be developed. A careful reading of this chapter, or better still of one of the books listed in its bibliography, is likely to be very helpful to anyone concerned with making such numbers as $-\frac{2}{3}$ and $\sqrt{2}$ meaningful to his pupils.

As we indicated in chapter 1, our possible objectives so far as number systems are concerned are: (1) manipulative skill in the standard work associated with the operations of addition, subtraction, multiplication and division, and the ordering relations on R, the set of real numbers, and its main subsets, (2) some insight into the structure associated with these number systems, (3) a well-developed feeling for the real number-line together with decimals, approximations, etc., (4) a picture (e.g. by Venn diagram) of the inter-relations of various sets of numbers, and familiarity with definitions, language and notation. Throughout we shall use the following notation:

N, the set of natural numbers $\{1, 2, 3, \dots\}$ (or positive integers),

W, the set of whole numbers $\{0, 1, 2, \dots\}$,

Z, the set of all integers $\{0, \pm 1, \pm 2, \dots\}$,

Q, the set of rational numbers $\left\{\dfrac{m}{n} : m \in Z, n \in N\right\}$,

Q^+, the set of positive rational numbers,

R, the set of real numbers,

C, the set of complex numbers.

(N, W, R, C are self-explanatory; Q is from quotient and Z from the German word Zahlen for number; Q^+ is, in many texts, used for the non-negative rational numbers.)

9.1. The Set of Natural Numbers *N*

The natural numbers are, of course, introduced at an early stage, starting with, say, the first 100 members and gradually building up the grasp of the fact that there is no largest natural number. Abstraction is preceded by counting collections of objects, matching such collections, etc., and by using sequences of symbols, such as:

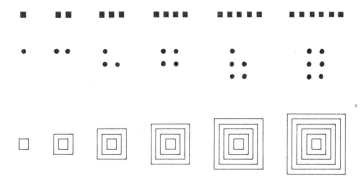

and so on.

These sequences essentially display Peano's axioms for *N*, which can be presented as follows:

(1) There is a first member.

(2) Given any member there is a next member (its "successor"), obtained by adding one symbol.

(3) The whole set is obtained from (1) and (2) (this leads to the principle of induction).

(4) The members are all different (the set is "infinite").

It is not suggested that these should be given to pupils, but merely that a flavour of the ideas can be set up with a suitable approach. For example, children take many years to appreciate the implications of (4): the set is infinite. This can be accentuated with early use of sequences such as the odd integers, the squares, the cubes, or the primes. The use of sequences which involve an obvious inductive step is particularly important. For example, the fact that

$$1+3+5+\ldots+(2n-1) = n^2 \qquad (n = 1, 2, 3 \ldots)$$

can be introduced early by building up the pattern

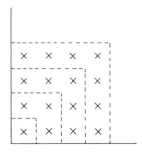

and noting that

$$
\begin{aligned}
1^2 &= 1 \\
2^2 &= 1+3 &&= 1^2+3 \\
3^2 &= 1+3+5 &&= 2^2+5 \\
4^2 &= 1+3+5+7 &&= 3^2+7
\end{aligned}
$$

. . . .

each square number arising from the preceding square number by adding the appropriate odd number, and each geometrical square arising from the preceding geometrical square by suitable bordering; each involves the main inductive step that, if the statement is true for the *k*th case, then it is true for the *next* case (the statement is also true for the *first* case).

Not even in the sixth form is it likely that a formal definition of the natural numbers will be asked for, but, if the teacher or a bright pupil is interested, a treatment based on Peano's axioms with inductive proofs of the properties of + and × will be found in such a book as *Algebraic Structures* by A. W. Bell (Allen and Unwin, 1966).

9.2. The Integers *Z*

The first opportunity for formal organization occurs after the introduction of the integers as described in chapter 5. The properties of addition, multiplication and ordering for integers can then be pointed out using special cases, and general statements can be made as the work proceeds and the necessary terms are introduced. It is helpful to present a table of the main properties in a summary.

Property	$+$	$\times$
closure	$a+b \in Z$	$a \times b \in Z$
commutative	$a+b = b+a$	$a \times b = b \times a$
associative	$a+(b+c) = (a+b)+c$	$a \times (b \times c) = (a \times b) \times c$
identity element	$a+0 = a$ (zero 0)	$a \times 1 = a$ (unity 1)
inverse elements	$a+(-a) = 0$	none (in general)
distributive	$a \times (b+c) = a \times b + a \times c$	

ordering: (i) one of $a < b, a = b, a > b$ holds;
    (ii) $a < b$ and $b < c \Rightarrow a < c$;
    (iii) $a < b \Rightarrow a+c < b+c$;
    (iv) $a < b \Rightarrow \begin{cases} ac < bc & \text{when } c > 0 \\ ac > bc & \text{when } c < 0. \end{cases}$

Other properties are: $a \times 0 = 0$; $a \times (-b) = -(a \times b)$; $(-a) \times (-b) = ab$;
$$a \times b = 0 \Rightarrow a = 0 \quad \text{or} \quad b = 0.$$

Also, every equation of the form $x+a = b$, where a, b are integers, has a unique integer solution, namely $x = b+(-a) = b-a$, in subtraction notation. It should be stressed that this result is one of the main advantages arising from the extension of whole numbers to integers; the equation $x+7 = 5$ has no whole-number solution, but has the integer solution -2.

One unpleasant feature in proceeding from the natural numbers to the integers is contained in the ordering property (iv);

in natural numbers, $a < b \Rightarrow ac < bc$ for all $c \in N$,

in integers, $a < b \Rightarrow \begin{cases} ac < bc & \text{when } c > 0 \\ ac > bc & \text{when } c < 0. \end{cases}$

This complication makes it harder to solve inequalities than to solve equations in integers.

THE CONSTRUCTION OF THE INTEGERS FROM THE NATURAL NUMBERS

Since the extension from N to Z has been introduced informally, we now show how to construct it by the use of "ordered pairs (a, b) of elements of N", that is, how to describe the integers and deduce their properties entirely in terms of the natural numbers and their properties. We do not now assume that negative integers exist. The clue lies in examining the set of all the equations of the type $x+a = b$ that are "equivalent"; e.g. $x+3 = 5$ is equivalent to each of the set of equations $x+1 = 3$, $x+2 = 4$, $x+3 = 5$, $x+4 = 6$, $x+5 = 7, \ldots$ since the same number has been added to each side, and all have the same solution, $x = 2$. If $x+a = b$ and $x+c = d$ are equations from this set, then $c-a = d-b$ (assuming $c > a$) and so $a+d = b+c$. Similarly $x+5 = 3$ is equivalent to each of the set of equations $x+3 = 1$, $x+4 = 2$, $x+5 = 3$, $x+6 = 4$, $x+7 = 5, \ldots$, but in this case there is no solution in N; we aim at extending N to a set in which there is a common solution ("-2"). Again, if $x+a = b$ and $x+c = d$ are equations from the set listed, then $a+d = b+c$.

This motivates the algebraic method of constructing Z, the set of integers, from N, the set of natural numbers. We consider the set $S = \{(a, b) : a, b \in N\}$ of all ordered pairs of elements of N (note that the equation $x + a = b$ involves an ordered pair (a, b) of elements of N) and define an equivalence relation on S by writing:

$$(a, b) \sim (c, d) \Leftrightarrow a + d = b + c.$$

This partitions S into equivalence classes and each equivalence class now represents an integer.

Addition, multiplication and ordering for integers are now *defined* by the addition, multiplication and ordering of equivalence classes:

$$[(a, b)] + [(c, d)] = [(a + c, b + d)]$$

$$[(a, b)] \times [(c, d)] = [(ac + bd, ad + bc)]$$

$$[(a, b)] < [(c, d)] \Leftrightarrow b + c < a + d$$

these definitions being motivated by thinking of (a, b) as $b - a$ and (c, d) as $d - c$. To complete the construction for the integers we have now to do the following:

(a) Check that the definitions for $+, \times$ and $<$ are independent of the choice of representatives, i.e. if $(a, b) \sim (a', b')$ and $(c, d) \sim (c', d')$, then

$$(a, b) + (c, d) = (a', b') + (c', d')$$

$$(a, b) \times (c, d) = (a', b') \times (c', d')$$

$$(a, b) < (c, d) \Leftrightarrow (a', b') < (c', d').$$

(b) Check that the subset of equivalence classes

$$\{[(1, a + 1)] : a \in N\}$$

can be identified with N.

(c) Check that the laws for Z (as listed) hold.

Note that as the construction is made, the natural numbers are *isomorphic* to a subset of these classes, i.e. they have the same properties. Thus the classes which represent the integers include the classes isomorphic to the natural numbers, and so in this sense

the integers include the natural numbers; it is often said that the integers Z include "a *copy* of" N.

This is a very formidable task! Some people are convinced that some of these ideas can be successfully given to pupils in the age range 11 to 16, but this is a most debatable view.

9.3. The Set of Positive Rationals (the extension $N \rightarrow Q^+$)

To construct Q^+ from N we proceed in very much the same way as for Z. We consider pairs of natural numbers a/b (conveniently written this way, because we shall identify this pair with the "fraction" $\dfrac{a}{b}$). If a, b have no common factor > 1, then the equation $bx = a$ is equivalent to each of the set of equations $\{tbx = ta : t \in N\}$, both sides having been multiplied by t, and all the equations have the unique solution

$$x = \frac{a}{b} \quad \left(\frac{a}{b} = \frac{2a}{2b} = \frac{3a}{3b} = \frac{4a}{4b} = \ldots \right).$$

We note that two fractions $\dfrac{a}{b}$ and $\dfrac{c}{d}$ are equivalent if and only if there are integers m, n such that $ma = nc$ and $mb = nd$, i.e. $ad = bc$.

The remarks motivate the algebraic method of constructing Q^+ from N by means of ordered pairs of elements of N. As for the extension $N \rightarrow Z$, we consider the set $S = \{(a/b) : a, b \in N\}$ of all ordered pairs of elements of N. (Note that the equation $bx = a$ involves an ordered pair (a/b) of elements of N.) In this case we define an equivalence relation on S by writing:

$$(a/b) \sim (c/d) \Leftrightarrow ad = bc.$$

This partitions S into equivalence classes, and each equivalence class now represents a rational number; the pair a/b in which a, b have HCF 1 is the representative of its class chosen to name the rational number a/b. In the use of the integer lattice in chapter 5 each equivalence class is represented by the set of lattice points (with positive coordinates) on the line of appropriate gradient, and the point nearest the origin gives its name to the class.

Addition, multiplication and ordering have now to be defined on the set of equivalence classes in a suitable way, and the facts verified that correspond to those listed for the extension of N to Z by means of the set S of ordered pairs of elements of N. Again this is a formidable task! Any teaching along these lines for 11- to 16-year-old pupils would require most careful presentation in order to be of any value.

9.4. The Set of All Rational Numbers (the extension $Z \to Q$)

Having obtained the set of all positive rational numbers, we can derive the set of all rational numbers by symmetry from the number-line. We first establish that for all $b \in N$, $0/b$ is neutral for addition and corresponds to 0; then that the negative rational number $-a/b$, the additive inverse of a/b,

is the number associated with the reflection in the origin of the point representing the positive rational number a/b. We then still have $a/b + c/b = (a+c)/b$ always, for all a, $c \in Z$ and all $b \in N$. The earlier work on operations and ordering for Z and Q^+ enables us to build up quickly the corresponding structure for Q. As for Z it is useful to present a table of the main facts for Q. Where "none (in general)" appears in the Z table in relation to the existence of a multiplicative inverse element, we now have for Q:

For each $a \in Q$, $a \neq 0$, $\exists a^{-1} \in Q$ such that $a \times a^{-1} = 1$.

It is worth pointing out at this stage that Q, the richest number system so far constructed, is an example of a *field* and that in it we can add, subtract, multiply and divide (except by zero).

We have clearly gained a great deal by our extensions $N \to Z \to Q$. Have we lost anything, and are there numbers on the number-line that are not in Q? In fact it is easier to deal with the second half of the question. At an early stage we meet, e.g. by the theorem of Pythagoras, a line segment of length $\sqrt{2}$ units. In a right-angled isosceles triangle with sides of length 1, the hypotenuse has length $\sqrt{2}$. By the usual argument, $\sqrt{2} \notin Q$. At this stage it is worth pointing out that $\sqrt{a}$, for each non-square $a \in N$, is not in Q. A construction that leads to line-segments of lengths $\sqrt{2}$, $\sqrt{3}$, $\sqrt{4} = 2$, $\sqrt{5}$, $\sqrt{6}, \ldots$ units can be presented as follows:

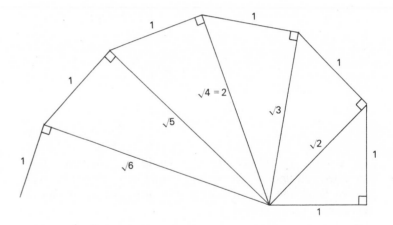

Another important non-rational number that the pupil meets at a fairly early stage is π. A line segment of length π units can be obtained by considering the diagram on page 90:

The number-line is placed as a tangent to the circle shown of radius 1, the origin O on the line being the point of contact. If we imagine the line wrapped round the circle, then the point corresponding to the number π coincides with the other end A of the diameter through O.

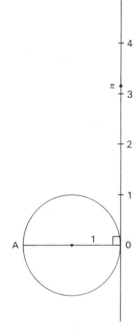

π is not in Q, but the proof of this is far from easy. Those interested can find an "elementary" proof in *Mathematical Analysis* by Scott and Tims (CUP), p. 459, or in *Calculus* by Spivak (Benjamin), p. 279, chapter 16.

9.5. The Real Number-Line; R, the Set of Real Numbers (the extension $Q \to R$)

So far we have described a number-line which has a unique point to represent each rational number and on which many irrational,

i.e. non-rational, numbers such as $\sqrt{2}$, $\sqrt{3}$, π, etc., can be represented. During the process of building up this collection of numbers we should be stressing that each such number is represented by a unique decimal which may be *finite* (and the number is then rational, e.g. $\frac{3}{4} = 0.75$), *infinite and periodic* (and the number is then also rational, e.g. $\frac{1}{3} = 0.33333\ldots = 0.\dot{3}$ (where $\dot{}$ means repeated); $\frac{1}{7} = 0.142857142857\ldots = 0.\dot{1}4285\dot{7}$, where the sequence of numbers 142857 is repeated infinitely often; $\frac{371}{12} = 30.91666\ldots = 30.91\dot{6}$), or *infinite and non-periodic* (and the number is then *irrational*, e.g. $\sqrt{2} = 1.41421356\ldots$, $\pi = 3.14159265\ldots$, etc.). We can always express a finite decimal as an infinite decimal, e.g. $0.75 = 0.75000\ldots = 0.75\dot{0}$.

Our remarks above lead to two of the usual simple ways of introducing the set R of real numbers: (1) as the set of all infinite decimals (with suitable identifications in special cases, e.g. $1.\dot{0} = 0.\dot{9}$), and (2) by means of the real number-line.

For (2) the assumption is made that every point corresponds to a unique real number, and that every real number corresponds to a unique point. This assumption is often called the *continuity* axiom for Euclidean geometry.

Addition, subtraction and ordering for R can clearly be illustrated by the number-line (as for Z and Q), but multiplication and division are more difficult.

We can give meaning to a product such as $\pi \times \sqrt{2}$ by considering the product of the infinite decimals representing π and $\sqrt{2}$; but, when we first meet these numbers, there is no harm in assuming that such a product exists and that we can approximate to it as closely as we like by means of decimals. Similarly in dealing with a quotient such as $\sqrt{2}/\pi$. All the basic properties of addition, subtraction, multiplication, division and order for Q do in fact go over to R, but there are several tiresome details involving limit

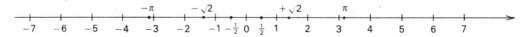

processes for infinite decimals which will need tidying up before they can be established; this is quite definitely university work.

It is clear, however, from work with university students that the continuum concept of the real numbers, even after an "A" Level course, has often not been built up. This is probably partly due to the "discrete" nature of many of the number activities of a practical nature that are met in school, such as pattern work with integers, division lines on rulers, and rational approximations in measuring. However, the situation can be improved by looking more closely at the relation between Q and R, and some of this work can start at the 11-to-16-age stage.

By considering the decimal expansion

$$\sqrt{2} = 1 \cdot 41421356 \ldots$$

we can produce a sequence of rational numbers

$$\{1, 1\cdot4, 1\cdot41, 1\cdot414, 1\cdot4142, 1\cdot41421, 1\cdot414213, \ldots\}$$

in increasing order of magnitude, each being a rational approximation to $\sqrt{2}$. This sequence of rational numbers has the irrational number $\sqrt{2}$ as "limit", a fact which illustrates a fundamental "topological" difference between Q and R. Q is not "complete", which means that it contains sequences which "converge" but not to elements of Q itself, whereas R is complete: every convergent sequence in R has its limit in R itself.

Using the same procedure as above for each $a \in R$ we can produce a sequence of rational numbers with a as limit. From these rational approximations it is clear that, given any $a \in R$, we can find a number $b \in Q$ as close to a as we please. We say that Q is *dense* in R.

As soon as teaching of calculus begins it can be pointed out that limit processes are possible over R but not over Q, so that calculus can be developed over R but not over Q.

THE EXTENSION $Q \to R$

One of the standard approaches starts with the set of all suitable sequences of elements of Q (so-called "Cauchy sequences") and with a suitable equivalence relation in this set; the sequences of rational approximations described above are Cauchy sequences.

There are many other methods of producing sequences of rational numbers that converge to limits in R and of obtaining "good" rational approximations to real numbers. Some of these are mentioned in chapters 6 and 10. For a further discussion of this see *From Graphs to Calculus*, a book in this series.

The set R of real numbers can be partitioned into two disjoint subsets: (1) the *algebraic* real numbers, (2) the *transcendental* (or non-algebraic) real numbers. An algebraic number satisfies a polynomial equation with rational coefficients (e.g. $\sqrt{2}$ is algebraic since it is a root of the polynomial equation $x^2 - 2 = 0$; every rational number a/b is algebraic since it satisfies $bx - a = 0$); a transcendental number satisfies no such equation (e.g. π is transcendental).

The number systems so far discussed can be illustrated by the following diagram in which a typical example of each type of number is given:

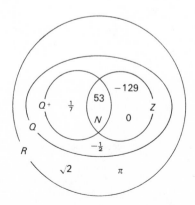

N natural numbers
$[W = N \cup \{0\}$ whole numbers$]$
Z integers
Q^+ positive rational numbers
Q rational numbers
R real numbers

9.6. The Set of Complex Numbers (the Extension $R \rightarrow C$)

Although the properties of complex numbers will not be discussed with most pupils until after the age of 16, they will usually have met problems which lead to the need for an extension of R. For example, they may have met quadratic equations with no roots in R such as $x^2 + 1 = 0$, $x^2 + x + 1 = 0$, etc. One approach is to define i by $i^2 = -1$ and take C as $\{a + ib : a, b \in R\}$ with R as the subset $\{a + i0 = a : a \in R\}$, and assume that addition and multiplication on C are defined in the usual way and satisfy the usual algebraic laws. This might be combined with the geometric view of complex numbers by means of the Argand diagram, which is equivalent to the geometric view of real numbers by means of the real number-line. Construction of C by means of ordered pairs of elements of R or 2×2 matrices over R of the form $\begin{pmatrix} a & -b \\ b & a \end{pmatrix}$ can be introduced at a later stage.

References

R is for Real, D. Wheeler, Open University Press.
The Same but Different, D. A. Quadling, Mathematical Association, Bell.
Algebra and Number Systems, J. Hunter *et al.*, Blackie/Chambers.

10 Investigations in Number Theory

10.0. Introduction

One of the objectives in teaching mathematics to pupils of age 14 or more must be to stimulate a sense of inquiry, discovery, conjecture and the imaginative thought processes leading to proof that is acceptable for the particular age involved.

Work in number is particularly suited for such activity and many topics can be, and in many cases have already been, built into the normal teaching of number over the whole age range 11 to 16, the presentation depending on the type of class and level of maturity involved. The main objectives for the use of this material in number might be listed as:

(1) To encourage exploratory and discovery work with number and at the same time to strengthen grasp of powers, divisors, operations, sequences, functions, etc.
(2) To develop a feeling for the truth or falsity of statements, the nature of a conjecture, the use of counter-examples and, where possible, the meaning of a suitable acceptable proof.
(3) To add variety to the teaching and learning situation and, by using a laboratory-type approach, to encourage initiative from pupils either individually, in small groups or in open classroom discussion.
(4) To introduce the pupil early to the fact that mathematics is still very much alive, by mentioning some of the easily described unsolved problems in number theory.

This chapter contains a large number of problems selected from a wide variety of topics in number. It is not intended to be exhaustive, but merely to indicate some of the ideas that might be used as starting points for pupil investigations, preparation of workcards or other forms of non-examinable teaching material. We feel that it would be wrong to attempt to develop each problem as far as possible; we prefer to take the view that teachers and pupils will wish to choose particular problems that interest them

and develop their own individual approach to a structure of investigation, question and answer for each such problem. However, it is reasonable to demand some indication of possible ways in which this work might be done, and we shall present a few developed situations in which a variety of points are considered, such as age and ability of pupil, mathematical prerequisites, nature of proof, levels of difficulty, integration into the normal curriculum.

Work of the type suggested is best dealt with in a "laboratory" setting, i.e. one in which personal or group activities of various types take place, ranging from guided routine practical work, through conjecture and discovery, to a suitable form of acceptable proof. Various aids to the activities should be available, such as geometrical instruments, materials for counting patterns and number bases, tables of many sorts, practical aids to calculation, graph paper of various types, an adequate supply of paper, pencils and pens of several colours, and other materials, including suitable reference books, that will be required as experience develops. It is certain that the majority of pupils will need clear guidance and in many cases explicit instructions; presentation in workcard form is therefore usually the best way of coping with the problems involved. Storage of materials has to be carefully organized and some form of workbook for each pupil or group of pupils is recommended. Our intention in this chapter is to provide a resource of number laboratory material for the teacher. Teachers who are interested in work of this nature that has already been prepared for a class should consult, for example, *Starting Points* by Banwell, Saunders and Tahta (OUP, 1972). The following investigations are there discussed in detail: p. 86 End digits, p. 88 Fractions, p. 102 Monodivisors, p. 108 Nine times table, p. 143 Sum of 100 numbers. Another similar source is the "Excursions" in

Pattern and Power of Mathematics by Moakes, Croome and Phillips (Macmillan).

10.1. Some Number Sequences

When sequences of numbers are first introduced it is important to stress that a sequence is uniquely determined only when we have a formula for the general nth term, or some rule for the construction of this term, and that it is not enough to provide the first few terms. For example, suppose that we have a sequence starting with $1, 2, 4, \ldots$; what are the next few terms and the general nth term? A question like this can lead to various types of useful classroom activity with pupils at different stages of development (see chapter 4) such as giving verbal descriptions of rules for forming sequences, discovering unusual sequences, obtaining a formula for the general nth term of a sequence, using a given formula to list the first 10 terms of a sequence, and so on. We list a few sequences all starting with $1, 2, 4, \ldots$:

(1) $1, 2, 4, 8, 16, \ldots$, i.e. $1, 2, 2^2, 2^3, 2^4, \ldots$, in which the general nth term is 2^{n-1} $(n = 1, 2, \ldots)$. In some senses this might be regarded as the "most natural" sequence of integers starting with $1, 2, 4, \ldots$.

(2) $1, 2, 4, 1, 2, 4, 1, 2, 4, \ldots$, in which $1, 2, 4$ are repeated in that order, so that the nth term is 1 when n is of the form $3m + 1$, 2 when n is of the form $3m + 2$, and 4 when n is of the form $3m$; we could also say more concisely that the nth term is $2^{n-1} \pmod 7$.

(3) $1, 2, 4, 3, 1, 2, 4, 3, \ldots$, in which $1, 2, 4, 3$ are repeated in that order, so that the $(n + 1)$th term is $2^n \pmod 5$.

(4) $1, 2, 4, 7, 11, 16, \ldots$, in which the differences between one term and the next term are $1, 2, 3, 4, 5, \ldots$, in turn, and the nth term is $\frac{1}{2}(n^2 - n + 2)$.

(5) $1, 2, 4, 5, 7, 8, 10, \ldots$, in which the successive differences between one term and the next term are $1, 2$ repeated in that order, and the nth term is $\frac{1}{2}(3n - 2)$ when n is even and $\frac{1}{2}(3n - 1)$ when n is odd.

(6) $1, 2, 4, 7, 8, 10, 13, 14, 16, 19, \ldots$, in which the successive differences between one term and the next term are $1, 2, 3$ repeated in that order, and the nth term is $2n - 1$ when n is of the form $3m + 1$ and $2n - 2$ when n is of the form $3m$ or $3m + 2$.

(7) $1, 2, 4, 10, 23, \ldots$, in which the nth term is $\frac{1}{2}(n^3 - 5n^2 + 10n - 4)$. Note that $\frac{1}{2}(n^3 - 5n^2 + 10n - 4) = \frac{1}{2}n^2(n - 5) + 5n - 2$, which can be seen to be always an integer on noting that either n^2 or $n - 5$ is even.

Clearly the list is endless, and some of the above results might be obtained by very few pupils in the age range 11 to 16. However, such activity should strengthen the grasp of ideas associated with the term "sequence".

I. SEQUENCES OF INTEGERS ASSOCIATED WITH GEOMETRICAL SHAPES

(1) *Triangular numbers*

Consider the sequence of integers

$$1, \quad 3 = 1 + 2, \quad 6 = 1 + 2 + 3, \quad 10 = 1 + 2 + 3 + 4,$$
$$15 = 1 + 2 + 3 + 4 + 5, \ldots,$$

in which the nth term is the sum $1 + 2 + 3 + \ldots + n$ of the first n natural numbers. This sequence can be represented by a sequence of dots as follows:

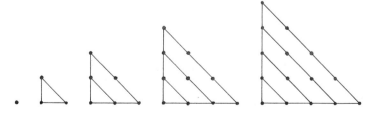

forming a sequence of right-angled triangles. For this reason these integers are usually called the *triangular numbers* and are often

denoted by T_n $(n = 1, 2, 3, \ldots)$; $T_1 = 1$, $T_2 = 3$, $T_3 = 6$, $T_4 = 10, \ldots$. Since $T_n = 1 + 2 + 3 + \ldots + n$ and $T_{n-1} = 1 + 2 + 3 + \ldots + (n-1)$ we see that $T_n = n + T_{n-1}$. This *recurrence* relation for T_n holds for $n = 2, 3, \ldots$, and for $n = 1$ also if we take $T_0 = 0$.

We can find a formula for T_n by building rectangles from the above sequence of triangles as follows:

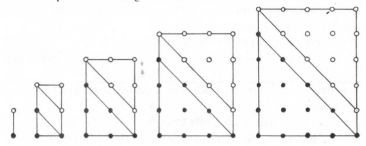

From symmetry and counting of dots, black and open,

$$2T_1 = 1 \times 2, \quad 2T_2 = 2 \times 3, \quad 2T_3 = 3 \times 4, \quad 2T_4 = 4 \times 5,$$
$$2T_5 = 5 \times 6, \ldots.$$

In general, $2T_n = n \times (n+1)$, so that $T_n = \frac{1}{2}n(n+1) = n\dfrac{n+1}{2}$

$= (n \times$ the mean of the first and last terms in the series
$$1 + 2 + 3 + \ldots + n).$$

Thus,
$$1 + 2 + 3 + \ldots + n = \tfrac{1}{2}n(n+1) \qquad (n = 1, 2, 3, \ldots)$$

In particular,
$$1 + 2 + 3 + \ldots + (n-1) = \tfrac{1}{2}(n-1)(n-1+1)$$
$$= \tfrac{1}{2}n(n-1) \qquad (n = 2, 3, \ldots)$$

Pupils could describe and try to explain the pattern of odd and even numbers in the sequence of triangular numbers.

Two interesting investigations involving triangular numbers can be presented as follows:

(i) Find the first four triangular numbers that are squares. (The set of such numbers is infinite.)

(ii) It has been shown that every positive integer is the sum of at most three triangular numbers. Compile a list expressing numbers in this way. "How many triangular numbers are prime numbers?", and other such questions can also be raised. Triangular numbers are recalled in the treatment of "combinations". The combination $\dbinom{n+1}{2}$, i.e. $(n+1)$ choose 2, is the nth triangular number and the "triangular" numbers appear in a diagonal line in Pascal's Triangle. There is further scope for investigation here.

$$
\begin{array}{c}
1 \\
1 \quad 1 \\
1 \quad 2 \quad \textcircled{1} \\
1 \quad 3 \quad \textcircled{3} \quad 1 \\
1 \quad 4 \quad \textcircled{6} \quad 4 \quad 1
\end{array}
$$

(2) *Isosceles numbers*

Consider the sequence of integers $1, 3 = 1 + 2, 7 = 1 + 2 + 4, 13 = 1 + 2 + 4 + 6, 21 = 1 + 2 + 4 + 6 + 8, \ldots$, in which the nth term is $1 + 2 + 4 + 6 + \ldots + 2(n-1) = 1 + 2\{1 + 2 + 3 + \ldots + (n-1)\}$. The sequence can be represented by the following sequence of dots:

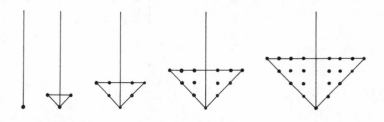

Since these form isosceles triangles (with the vertex as the only point on the axis of symmetry), we could call the numbers *isosceles numbers* and denote them by I_n $(n = 1, 2, \ldots)$. From the diagrams it is clear that $I_n = 1 + 2T_{n-1} (n = 1, 2, \ldots)$ (taking $T_0 = 0$ as before), giving a relation between the triangular numbers and the isosceles numbers. This relation was already obvious from the formula $I_n = 1 + 2\{1 + 2 + 3 + \ldots + (n-1)\}$; from this we obtain:

$$I_n = 1 + 2 \cdot \tfrac{1}{2}n(n-1) = n^2 - n + 1 \qquad (n = 1, 2, \ldots).$$

As with triangular numbers, various investigations on properties of isosceles numbers can be raised such as:

(i) Obtain the recurrence relation connecting I_n and I_{n-1}
$$(I_n = 2(n-1) + I_{n-1}).$$

(ii) Explain why every isosceles number is odd.

(iii) Find the isosceles numbers < 1000 that are also triangular numbers.

(iv) The only isosceles number that is a square is $I_1 = 1 = 1^2$. (It would be of interest to see if any pupils could devise a proof of this fact such as:

For $n \geqslant 1$, $(n-1)^2 = n^2 - 2n + 1 < n^2 - n + 1 \leqslant n^2$, and so
$$(n-1)^2 < I_n \leqslant n^2.$$

Thus I_n is sandwiched between the neighbouring squares $(n-1)^2$ and n^2 and so I_n is a square if and only if $n^2 - n + 1 = n^2$, i.e. if and only if $n = 1$.)

(v) It can be proved that the only possible prime factors of isosceles numbers are 3 and primes of the form $6k + 1$ (e.g. 7, 13, 19, 31, 37, 43, $\ldots$, and not 5, 11, 17, $\ldots$). Investigate the prime factors of, say, the first thirty isosceles numbers.

(3) *Equiangular numbers*

Consider the sequence of integers $1, 4 = 1 + 3, 10 = 1 + 3 + 6, 19 = 1 + 3 + 6 + 9, 31 = 1 + 3 + 6 + 9 + 12, \ldots$, in which the nth term is $1 + 3 + 6 + 9 + \ldots + 3(n-1) = 1 + 3\{1 + 2 + 3 + \ldots + (n-1)\}$. The sequence can be represented by the sequence of dots at the foot of the page:

Since these form equiangular triangles we could call the numbers *equiangular numbers* and denote them by E_n $(n = 1, 2, 3, \ldots)$. From the series for E_n, it is clear that $E_n = 1 + 3T_{n-1}$, giving a relation between the equiangular numbers and the triangular numbers. Also $E_n = 1 + \tfrac{3}{2}(I_n - 1) = \tfrac{1}{2}(3I_n - 1)$, providing a formula connecting the equiangular and the isosceles numbers. Further,

$$E_n = 1 + 3\{1 + 2 + 3 + \ldots + (n-1)\}$$
$$= 1 + \tfrac{3}{2}n(n-1) = \tfrac{1}{2}(3n^2 - 3n + 2) \quad (n = 1, 2, \ldots).$$

 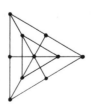 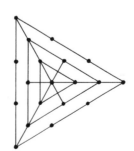 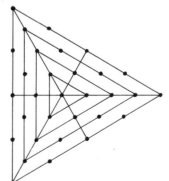

Some activities for equiangular numbers could be:

(i) Obtain the recurrence relation connecting E_n and E_{n-1}.

(ii) Describe and explain the pattern of odd and even numbers in the sequence.

(iii) For the first thirty equiangular numbers, find those that are squares or cubes, and those that are primes, and list the different primes that occur as factors of these thirty numbers. Which numbers are triangular numbers or isosceles numbers?

(4) Rhombic numbers

These are the integers in the sequence 1, $5 = 1+4$, $13 = 1+4+8$, $25 = 1+4+8+12$, $41 = 1+4+8+12+16,\ldots$, in which the nth term is $1+4+8+12+ \ldots +4(n-1) = 1+4\{1+2+3+ \ldots +(n-1)\} = 2n^2 - 2n + 1$.

The sequence can be represented by a sequence of dots as shown opposite:

The numbers are often called *rhombic numbers* because of the rhombic figures involved and denoted by R_n $(n = 1, 2, 3, \ldots)$. Some of the investigations that we could carry out for these numbers are:

(i) Explain why every rhombic number is odd.

(ii) List the first thirty rhombic numbers and find those that are squares, cubes, triangular numbers, isosceles numbers or equiangular numbers.

(iii) List all the primes that occur as factors of these numbers and check that they are all of the form $4k+1$. It can be proved that all prime factors of rhombic numbers are of this type, so that, for example, no rhombic number is divisible by 3.

(iv.) Check that the end digit of each of the first thirty rhombic numbers is 1, 3 or 5. These are the possible end digits for all rhombic numbers; try to prove this. (This can be established by forming a table of end digits as follows:

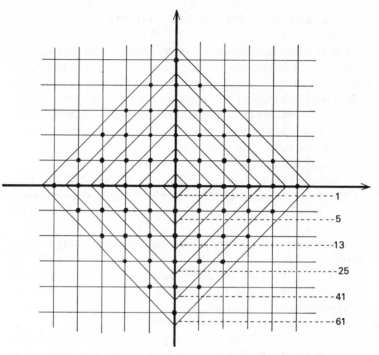

n	1	2	3	4	5	6	7	8	9	0
$-2n$	-2	-4	-6	-8	-10	-12	-14	-16	-18	0
$2n^2$	2	8	18	32	50	72	98	128	162	0
$2n^2 - 2n + 1$	1	5	3	5	1	1	5	3	5	1

The last line of the table shows that the end digits occur cyclically in the order 1 5 3 5 1 in the sequence.)

(5) Pentagonal numbers

These are the numbers in the sequence 1, $6 = 1+5$, $16 = 1+5+10$, $31 = 1+5+10+15$, $51 = 1+5+10+15+20,\ldots$, in which the nth term is $1+5\{1+2+3+\ldots+(n-1)\} = \frac{1}{2}(5n^2-5n+2)$ $(n=1,2,3,\ldots)$.

The numbers can be represented by a sequence of dots forming pentagons in layers and, for this reason, can be denoted by P_n $(n=1,2,3,\ldots)$ and called *pentagonal numbers*. Able pupils could be asked to sketch the first 5 or 6 pentagons. Just as for the rhombic and other numbers already described, various investigations on odd and even numbers, overlap with other number sequences, end digits, prime factors, etc., can be set.

(6) *Hexagonal numbers*

These are the numbers in the sequence $1, 7 = 1+6, 19 = 1+6 +12, 37 = 1+6+12+18, 61 = 1+6+12+18+24,\ldots$, in which the nth term is $1+6\{1+2+3+\ldots+(n-1)\} = 3n^2-3n+1$ $(n=1,2,3,\ldots)$.

In this case the numbers can be represented by dots forming layers of hexagons and the numbers are denoted by H_n $(n=1,2,3,\ldots)$. Again the pupils could be asked to sketch the first few hexagons and to investigate some listed properties of hexagonal numbers such as:

    (i) Explain why hexagonal numbers are odd.

    (ii) List the first thirty hexagonal numbers and check any overlap with the number sequences already introduced.

    (iii) List the primes that occur as prime factors and check that all are of the form $6k+1$. (Compare the corresponding result for isosceles numbers.) It can be proved that only primes of this form can occur as prime factors of hexagonal numbers. Explain why it is obvious that 3 cannot be a factor of H_n for any $n \geqslant 1$.

    (iv) Check that the end digits of H_n $(n=1,2,3,\ldots)$ occur cyclically in the order 1, 7, 9, 7, 1. Try to explain this result.

Clearly we have been considering sequences of integers of a common type in which the nth term is $1+k\{1+2+3+\ldots+ (n-1)\} = \frac{1}{2}(kn^2-kn+2)$ $(n=1,2,3,\ldots)$; for $k=2,3,4,5,6,\ldots$, we have isosceles, equiangular, rhombic, pentagonal, hexagonal,$\ldots$

numbers. We have indicated some of the properties of these sequences and some of the investigations that can be suggested for classroom or general-interest activity. The form of presentation for pupils will clearly depend on the age, ability and experience of the pupils concerned. When the idea of a sequence is being introduced it might be enough to concentrate on the geometrical patterns, and some of the work on even or odd numbers and prime factors. Then later the nth-term formulae can be used and relations between the sequences and the form of the end digits investigated. Pupils should be encouraged to discover other facts about the sequences. At some stage it might be of interest to point out that for each sequence the nth term is of the form an^2+bn+c, where the constants, a, b, c, are integers or rational numbers (in fact $\frac{1}{2} \times$ an odd integer, for the cases considered), and that the second differences for such sequences are constant. For example, for the rhombic numbers R_n we have:

Pupils could be encouraged at a suitable stage to use the converse situation, i.e. given constant second differences, to obtain the expression an^2+bn+c for the nth term by solving the three linear equations in a, b, c, arising from $n=1,2,3$.

(For completeness we include an indication of how the facts about the prime factors of $I_n = n^2-n+1$ $(n=1,2,\ldots)$ can be established. If p is a prime factor of I_n, then $n^2-n+1 \equiv 0$ (mod p). Thus $4n^2-4n+4 \equiv 0$ (mod p)$(p \neq 2)$ and so $(2n-1)^2 \equiv -3$ (mod p). Hence either $p = 3$ or $\left(\dfrac{-3}{p}\right) = +1$, where $\left(\dfrac{-3}{p}\right)$ is the Legendre symbol.* It follows that $p \equiv 1$ (mod 6), i.e. that p is of the form $6k+1$.

* See H. Davenport, *The Higher Arithmetic*, Hutchinson University Library, 1970, p. 65.

Quadratic residues can be used to obtain corresponding results for other sequences of the type described.)

II. FURTHER SEQUENCES OF INTEGERS ASSOCIATED WITH GEOMETRICAL SHAPES

The sequences just described could be called "2-dimensional" in the sense that they can be represented by 2-dimensional patterns and have nth terms of second degree of the form $an^2 + bn + c$. Many interesting sequences are "3-dimensional" in that they can be represented by 3-dimensional patterns, have nth terms of the form $an^3 + bn^2 + cn + d$ and give rise to constant third differences. We consider two of these.

(1) Tetrahedral numbers

These are the integers in the sequence 1, $4 = 1 + 3$, $10 = 1 + 3 + 6$, $20 = 1 + 3 + 6 + 10$, $35 = 1 + 3 + 6 + 10 + 15, \ldots$, in which the nth term is the sum of the first n triangular numbers. These numbers can be represented by points on or inside a sequence of tetrahedra as follows, and for this reason are called *tetrahedral numbers*:

Some activities for such numbers could be:

(i) List the first twenty tetrahedral numbers.

(ii) Determine which of these are also triangular numbers. (It is an unproved conjecture that the set of such numbers is infinite.)

(iii) Verify that the nth tetrahedral number is $\frac{1}{6}n(n+1)(n+2)$, for $1 \leqslant n \leqslant 20$. At a suitable stage it could be shown that the number is

$$\sum_{r=1}^{n} T_r = \sum_{r=1}^{n} \tfrac{1}{2}r(r+1) = \tfrac{1}{2}\sum_{r=1}^{n} r^2 + \tfrac{1}{2}\sum_{r=1}^{n} r$$

$$= \tfrac{1}{2} \cdot \tfrac{1}{6}n(n+1)(2n+1) + \tfrac{1}{2} \cdot \tfrac{1}{2}n(n+1)$$

$$= \tfrac{1}{6}n(n+1)(n+2)$$

(iv) Investigate how to represent tetrahedral numbers by using practical space material.

(v) Verify that the third-order differences are constant.

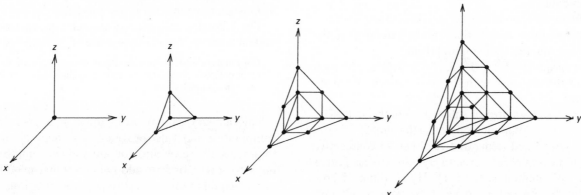

(2) *Pyramidal numbers*

These numbers arise from the numbers of identical balls that can be stacked in square pyramids with $1, 2, 3, \ldots$ layers. The numbers are 1, $5 = 1+4$, $14 = 1+4+9$, $30 = 1+4+9+16$, $55 = 1+4+9+16+25, \ldots$, the nth number being $1^2 + 2^2 + 3^2 + \ldots + n^2$.

Again, various investigations can be devised for these numbers such as finding the only two that are squares, showing that the third differences are constant, and checking that the nth number is $\frac{1}{6}n(n+1)(2n+1)$.

III. THE FIBONACCI SEQUENCE

One of the many interesting sequences of integers that can be introduced in the age range 11 to 16 (or earlier) is the well-known Fibonacci sequence

$$1, 1, 2, 3, 5, 8, 13, \ldots$$

which is formed by the rule that each number after the second is the sum of the two preceding numbers. Different sequences arise using different choices for the first two numbers.

Some activities could be:

(i) List the first twenty members (at least) of the sequence.

(ii) It was proved quite recently that only two numbers in the sequence are squares. Can you find them?

(iii) Form the products 1×2, 1×3, 2×5, $3 \times 8, \ldots$ of each number in the sequence with the next-but-one. What do you notice?

(iv) Form the sum of squares of successive numbers: $1^2 + 1^2$, $1^2 + 2^2$, $2^2 + 3^2 \ldots$. What do you notice this time?

(v) Verify for your listed terms that each pair of consecutive integers in the sequence are relatively prime to each other (i.e. have no common factor > 1). Try to think of how this might be proved in general by a contradiction argument. (This difficult argument could be presented as follows: "Suppose that $d \, (>1)$ is a common divisor of U_n

and U_{n+1}, two neighbouring terms of this sequence, U_n denoting the nth term. Now $U_{n+1} = U_n + U_{n-1}$, so that $U_{n-1} = U_{n+1} - U_n$. Since d is a divisor of U_n and U_{n+1} it is also a divisor of $U_{n+1} - U_n$ and so of U_{n-1}. From the fact that d is a divisor of U_n and U_{n-1} we can show similarly that d divides U_{n-2}. Proceeding backwards in this way it follows that d divides $U_1 = 1$. Since $d > 1$ we have a contradiction and the result follows.)

The results suggested by (iii) and (iv) are proved without too much difficulty by induction. (To establish (iv), take $U_{2n} = U_n(U_{n+1} + U_{n-1})$ and $U_{2n+1} = U_n^2 + U_{n+1}^2$ together.)

IV. SOME INTERESTING NUMBER CHAINS (FINITE SEQUENCES)

We add a few further comments here on the problem already discussed in 8.4 and 4.4. Start with any whole number and form a chain by the following rules:

(1) If a number is even, divide it by 2.

(2) If a number is odd, multiply it by 3 and add 1.

Stop when the number 1 is first reached.

The following collection of instructions, questions, comments and facts arose from classroom use of this number chain process.

> Copy and complete the number chain which starts with the number 17. Make other complete chains starting with other numbers < 100. What is the longest chain that you have found?

This activity can involve pupils in a great deal of simple computation and it also provides, for some, a valuable opportunity to practice the recognition of odd and even numbers. A common pupil error is to forget to add 1 after trebling an odd number and it seems helpful in this context to pose the questions:

> What sort of number follows an odd number in a chain?
> What sort of number follows an even number in a chain?

so that pupils become convinced that

$$\text{odd} \rightarrow \text{even}$$

but

$$\text{even} \rightarrow \text{even or odd.}$$

The completed chain starting with 17 is

$$17 \rightarrow 52 \rightarrow 26 \rightarrow 13 \rightarrow 40 \rightarrow 20 \rightarrow 10 \rightarrow 5 \rightarrow 16 \rightarrow 8 \rightarrow 4 \rightarrow 2 \rightarrow 1$$

and we can say that the chain starting with 17 takes 12 steps to reach 1. Some numbers produce very long chains, an outstanding example being 27, which generates a chain with 111 steps and approaches 10 000 on the way. In contrast, 96 generates a chain with only 12 steps and the chain generated by the nth power of 2, 2^n, has n steps (e.g. $4 \rightarrow 2 \rightarrow 1$). The unexpected variety and apparent unpredictability helps to make this situation an interesting one. The other two-digit numbers that produce chains with more than 90 steps are 31, 41, 47, 54, 55, 62, 63, 71, 73, 82, 83, 91, 94, 95, 97. All the remaining two-digit numbers generate chains of 35 steps or less.

In an attempt to produce longer chains, pupils sometimes extend them backwards and this produces a potentially interesting situation to investigate. For example, the one number which can immediately precede 24 in a chain is 48, but 16 has two possible predecessors, 5 or 32. Many pupils will respond to the challenge of finding other numbers with two predecessors and the sequence may emerge: 4, 10, 16, 22, 28 ... (odd multiples of 3 increased by 1). The ultimate outcome of this investigation could be a number tree growing from 1 and branching at the numbers in the above sequence. (A large sheet of paper is needed for this activity!)

Although it is a relatively easy matter to confirm that all two-digit numbers produce chains which ultimately reach 1, the more-general question as to whether every number generates a chain which eventually reaches 1 is, so far as we know, unanswered. Consequently this activity confronts pupils with an easily de-scribed conjecture which still awaits proof or rejection by counter-example.

Finally pupils could be encouraged to invent their own rules for forming number chains (or sequences) and to investigate the results.

10.2. Some Interesting Results for Numbers Involving Patterns, Series, Divisors

We collect under several headings various activities that can be presented to pupils in the age range 11 to 16 in ways depending on the ages, abilities and knowledge involved.

I. PATTERNS

(1) Investigate and continue the following pattern of corresponding equalities:

$$2 \times 2 = 4 \qquad\qquad 2 + 2 = 4$$
$$\tfrac{3}{2} \times 3 = 4\tfrac{1}{2} \qquad\qquad \tfrac{3}{2} + 3 = 4\tfrac{1}{2}$$
$$\tfrac{4}{3} \times 4 = 5\tfrac{1}{3} \qquad\qquad \tfrac{4}{3} + 4 = 5\tfrac{1}{3}$$
$$\tfrac{5}{4} \times 5 = 6\tfrac{1}{4} \qquad\qquad \tfrac{5}{4} + 5 = 6\tfrac{1}{4}$$
$$? = ? \qquad\qquad\qquad ? = ?$$

What is the nth line for each column, and why do $\times$ and $+$ give the same result?

(2) *Magic Squares*

(Square arrays of numbers in which the rows, columns and two main diagonals add to the same total.) Check that

4	9	2
3	5	7
8	1	6

is a magic square. It was known at least as early as 1000 BC.

Indicate how new magic squares can be obtained by addition or subtraction of numbers, etc.

Complete the following to form magic squares:

15		11
	9	
		3

14		
	8	
		2

16		2	13
	10		
		7	
4			1

1			12
	4		
	5	16	
8			13

Pupils may have difficulty with the 4×4 squares.

II. SERIES

For each of the following, complete and continue the equations given. Try to form the general nth equation in each case, and investigate the possibility of producing some type of proof of the result involved, e.g. by patterns of dots, by algebra or by induction for any pupils who can master this process.

$$
\begin{aligned}
(1) \qquad 1 &= 1^2 \\
1+3 &= 2^2 \\
1+3+5 &= ? \\
1+3+5+7 &= ?
\end{aligned}
$$

(In this case, squares of dots can "prove" that

$$1+3+5+ \ldots +(2n-1) = n^2.)$$

$$
\begin{aligned}
(2) \qquad 1 &= ? \\
3+5 &= ? \\
7+9+11 &= ? \\
13+15+17+19 &= ?
\end{aligned}
$$

Most pupils will obtain:

$$
\begin{aligned}
1 &= 1^3 \\
3+5 &= 2^3 \\
7+9+11 &= 3^3 \\
13+15+17+19 &= 4^3 \\
21+23+25+27+29 &= 5^3, \text{etc.,}
\end{aligned}
$$

and probably note that, when n^3 is on the right-hand side, there are n odd integers on the left-hand side.

It is not so obvious that the first n equations have $1+2+3+\ldots+n = \frac{1}{2}n(n+1)$ odd integers in all on their left-hand sides, so that the last such integer is $2 \times \frac{1}{2}n(n+1)-1$, i.e. n^2+n-1. Thus the nth equation is

$$(n^2-n+1)+(n^2-n+3)+ \ldots +(n^2+n-3)+(n^2+n-1) = n^3, {}^*$$

the first number (i.e. n^2-n+1) being $(n^2+n-1)-2(n-1)$.

A proof that (*) is true can be obtained in several ways; e.g. left-hand side $= \{1+3+5+\ldots+(n^2+n-1)\}$

$$-\{1+3+5+\ldots+(n^2-n-1)\}$$

$$= \{\tfrac{1}{2}(n^2+n)\}^2 - \{\tfrac{1}{2}(n^2-n)\}^2,$$

using Problem (1) above

$$= n^3.$$

Clearly the algebraic work is suitable, if at all, only for older and able pupils. The following shorter proof is probably a little more sophisticated but much more satisfying. We rewrite the equations as

$$
\begin{aligned}
1 &= 1^3 \\
(2^2-1)+(2^2+1) &= 2^3 \\
(3^2-2)+3^2+(3^2+2) &= 3^3
\end{aligned}
$$

then we want to show that the average number in the nth row is n^2. Since there are n numbers, then the sum of each row is n^3.

$$(3) \quad (1+2)^2 = 9 = 1^3+2^3$$
$$(1+2+3)^2 = 36 = 1^3+2^3+3^3$$
$$(1+2+3+4)^2 = 100 = 1^3+2^3+3^3+4^3$$
$$? = ? = ?$$

$$(4) \quad 1^2+2^2 = 3^2-2^2$$
$$2^2+3^2 = 7^2-6^2$$
$$3^2+4^2 = 13^2-12^2$$
$$4^2+5^2 = 21^2-20^2$$
$$? = ?$$

$$(5) \quad 2^2(2^3-1) = 1^3+3^3$$
$$2^4(2^5-1) = 1^3+3^3+5^3+7^3$$
$$2^6(2^7-1) = 1^3+3^3+5^3+7^3+9^3+11^3+13^3+15^3$$
$$? = ?$$

$$(6) \quad 3^2+4^2 = 5^2$$
$$10^2+11^2+12^2 = 13^2+14^2$$
$$21^2+22^2+23^2+24^2 = 25^2+26^2+27^2$$
$$36^2+37^2+38^2+39^2+40^2 = 41^2+42^2+43^2+44^2$$
$$? = ?$$

III. DIVISORS

We list some work on divisors of numbers that should help to consolidate the ideas involved. Some of the activities can be given quite early, but others require greater maturity.

(1) Perfect, deficient and abundant numbers

A positive integer (>1) is called *perfect* if it is equal to the sum of its proper divisors (i.e. positive divisors less than itself); e.g. $28 = 1+2+4+7+14$.

If the sum of the proper divisors is smaller the number is called *deficient*; e.g. $45 > 1+3+5+9+15$.

If the sum of the proper divisors is greater the number is called *abundant*; e.g. $12 < 1+2+3+4+6$.

Classify the integers from 1 to 100.

(i) Is it always true that the sum of two numbers of the same type is again of that type?

(ii) Is it always true that the product of two numbers of the same type is again of that type?

(iii) Is every multiple of a number of a given type again of that type?

(iv) Is every integer of the form $6k$ $(k \geqslant 2)$ abundant? (6 is perfect).

(v) Show that $2^{\alpha}p$, where $\alpha \geqslant 2$ and p is an odd prime, is abundant if and only if $p < 2^{\alpha+1}-1$.

Try to raise other questions for this classification of integers.

In proving (i), (ii), (iii) the most difficult task is probably that of showing that if n is abundant so is kn for each integer $k \geqslant 1$.

For (iv), it is enough to note that $1, k, 2k, 3k$ are distinct proper divisors of $6k$ and their sum is $1+k(1+2+3) > 6k$.

For (v), the proper divisors of $2^{\alpha}p$ are $1, p; 2, 2p; 2^2, 2^2p; \ldots, 2^{\alpha-1}, 2^{\alpha-1}p; 2^{\alpha}$ and their sum is

$$(1+2+ \ldots +2^{\alpha})+(1+2+ \ldots +2^{\alpha-1})p$$
$$= (2^{\alpha+1}-1)+(2^{\alpha}-1)p = (2^{\alpha+1}-1)-p+2^{\alpha}p.$$

It follows that $2^{\alpha}p$ is abundant if and only if $(2^{\alpha+1}-1)-p > 0$, i.e. $p < 2^{\alpha+1}-1$; (e.g. $4 \times 5 = 20$ is abundant, whereas $4 \times 7 = 28$ is not).

(2) Some division problems

(a) Find the smallest odd integer $n \geqslant 5$ for which $3|n, 5|(n+2)$ and $7|(n+4)$. ($a|b$ means: "a divides b".)

(b) Find the smallest positive integer n for which

(i) each of n, $n+1$ and $n+2$ has a square factor,

(ii) $n = 2x^2 = 3y^3 = 5z^5$ for some integers x, y, z,

(iii) $3^2|n$, $4^2|(n+1)$ and $5^2|(n+2)$,

(iv) $2|n$, $3|(n+1)$, $4|(n+2)$, $5|(n+3)$ and $6|(n+4)$, $(n > 2)$.

IV. INTEGERS AS MULTIPLES OF TWO GIVEN INTEGERS; THREES AND FIVES

The following diagram shows a train of 3-rods and 5-rods:

It is 19 units long.
What other lengths, up to 40, say, can you make with 3s and 5s?
Try another pair of rods. What lengths can you make by putting them end to end?

This is a situation which provides useful routine computational experience, together with an opportunity for pupils to invent some strategies which can lead towards ideas of generalization and proof. When tried with pupils the following statements were produced:

(i) I have made 14 (with 3s and 5s) and by doubling I can get 28.
(ii) I can add together the ways of making 17 and 14 to make 31.
(iii) I can only get even numbers if I use 6s and 8s.

The only lengths that cannot be made with 3s and 5s are 1, 2, 4 and 7. This can be seen by listing multiples of 3 and multiples of 5 separately, and then using the lists systematically. All lengths bigger than 7 can be made with 3s and 5s, but it is not easy for pupils to see this in an acceptable way. However, using the idea in (ii) above, it is easy to see that every length above 40 (the upper limit used for the initial numerical investigation) can be obtained from 3s and 5s.

In fact the following general results are true (see H. A. Fay, *Mathematical Gazette* 59, pp. 154 f. (1975)):

(i) If p and q are coprime (i.e., the HCF of p and q is 1), then the largest length that cannot be made with ps and qs is $pq-(p+q)$.
(ii) If p and q are coprime then there are $\frac{1}{2}(p-1)(q-1)$ different lengths that cannot be made with ps and qs.
(iii) If p and q are *not* coprime, then the lengths that can be made form a subset of the multiples of the HCF of p and q.

As special cases we have the following:

With 5s and 7s we *cannot* make the lengths 1, 2, 3, 4, 6, 8, 9, 11, 13, 16, 18, 23; here $p = 5$, $q = 7$, the list has $12 = \frac{1}{2}(p-1)(q-1)$ members and the largest is $23 = pq-(p+q)$.

With 9s and 15s, we can make 9, 15, 18, 24, 27, 30, ...

For a given choice of p and q, some numbers can be constructed in several different ways, but uniqueness can be obtained by choosing the representation with the maximum number of the smaller length rods. With 3s and 5s this convention leads to the following table:

Number	3s	5s	Number	3s	5s
3	1	0	12	4	0
5	0	1	13	1	2
6	2	0	14	3	1
8	1	1	15	5	0
9	3	0	16	2	2
10	0	2	17	4	1
11	2	1	18	·6	0

For this type of activity, structural apparatus (e.g. Cuisenaire rods) may be useful.

The answers to the following questions can be demonstrated informally in the classroom as indicated in the following work.

What is the largest integer length that *cannot* be made up, using a combination of 3-rods and 5-rods? How many integer lengths cannot be made up in this way? Which integer lengths can be *made up in several ways*?

Table of values for the trains

Number of fives						
3	15	18	21	24	27	30
2	10	13	16	19	22	25
1	5	8	11	14	17	20
0	0	3	6	9	12	15
	0	1	2	3	4	5 Number of threes

We put these values at the points of a lattice as follows:

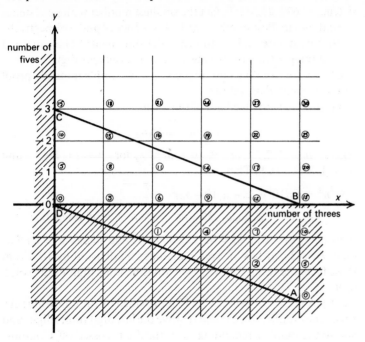

We wish to know which numbers can be represented by 3s and 5s (using positive integer multiples). These are the numbers in the unshaded part of the lattice.

A number can be represented in several ways, e.g. when 3 fives are replaced by 5 threes and vice versa. We notice on the lattice diagram that points which represent the same number n lie on a line $3x + 5y = n$. Two points which represent the same number must therefore be joined by an integer multiple of the vector $(+5, -3)$.

We now consider the parallelogram OABC (excluding the sides AB and BC). Inside and on this parallelogram are 15 lattice points,

representing the integers from 0 to 14. Since this parallelogram can contain no vector $(+5, -3)$, each of the integers 0 to 14 must be represented exactly once.

We now see that the largest integer that cannot be made up in threes and fives is $7 = 15 - 5 - 3$. In general for ps and qs, this is $pq - p - q$. We can also see how many values cannot be made up. There are 4, i.e. 1, 2, 4, 7. In general there are $\frac{1}{2}(p-1)(q-1)$. Finally, with the exception of 16, 17, 19 and 22, all the integers exceeding 14 can be made up in several different ways (the exceptions correspond to 1, 2, 4 and 7).

10.3. Problems Involving Decimal and Other Bases; Digits

In this section we gather together various problems concerned mainly with digits in number bases, especially the ordinary decimal base. Unlike the problems in 10.1 and 10.2, the problems here are given with little or no comment, and so will require to be developed for classroom use; such development can be helped by pilot use with suitable classes.

(1) By hand or by a calculator of some kind investigate the following patterns of digits:

(a)
$$\begin{aligned}
7 \times 7 &= 49 \\
67 \times 67 &= 4489 \\
667 \times 667 &= 444889 \\
6667 \times 6667 &= 44448889 \\
? &= ?
\end{aligned}$$

(b)
$$\begin{aligned}
4 \times 4 &= 16 \\
34 \times 34 &= 1156 \\
334 \times 334 &= 111556 \\
3334 \times 3334 &= 11115556 \\
? &= ?
\end{aligned}$$

(c)
$$\begin{aligned}
9 \times 9 &= 81 \\
99 \times 99 &= 9801 \\
999 \times 999 &= 998001 \\
9999 \times 9999 &= 99980001 \\
? &= ?
\end{aligned}$$

Can you find any other such patterns?

(2) Investigate the digits of the numbers: 1^2, 11^2, 111^2, 1111^2, etc.

(3) Investigate the patterns:

(a)
$$(1 \times 9) + 2 = 11$$
$$(12 \times 9) + 3 = 111$$
$$(123 \times 9) + 4 = 1111$$
$$(1234 \times 9) + 5 = 11111$$
$$? = ?$$

(Try to explain this.)

(b)
$$(8 \times 1) + 1 = 9$$
$$(8 \times 12) + 2 = 98$$
$$(8 \times 123) + 3 = 987$$
$$? = ?$$

(4) Form successive multiples $1 \times$, $2 \times$, $3 \times, \ldots$ of each of the integers (a) 142857, (b) 12345679, (c) 123456789, (d) 987654321, and comment on any interesting properties that you notice.

(5) Choose any 1-digit number. Multiply it by 3, then the result by 7, then that result by 11, then that result by 13 and finally that result by 37. Can you explain the result obtained?

(6) Choose any 3-digit number. Multiply it by 7; multiply the answer by 11; multiply that answer by 13. Perform this for several such numbers. Try to explain what happens.

(7) Numbers are transformed by summing the cubes of the digits, e.g.:

$$122 \to 1 + 8 + 8 = 17 \to 1 + 343 = 344, \text{ etc.}$$

Investigate the sequences which result. Is there any peculiarity when starting with multiples of 3?

(8) Numbers are transformed by multiplying their digits, e.g.:

$$679 \to 378 \to 168 \to 48 \to 32 \to 6.$$

It seems that wherever we start we ultimately arrive at a single-digit number. Try to prove this.

The number of steps involved in this process for any given number is called the *persistence* of the number. Thus the persistence of 679 is 5. It is in fact the smallest number with persistence 5. Find the smallest numbers with persistences 4 and 6 respectively.

(9) Investigate and try to prove the statement: "The square of an odd integer (to base 10) always has an *even* tens digit".

Clearly we can take odd integers $\geqslant 5$. A "simple minded" proof can be presented as follows.

The integers involved are of the form

$$n = a_k \ldots a_2 a_1 a_0$$

where $a_k = 1, 2, \ldots,$ or 9, $0 \leqslant a_i \leqslant 9$ for $1 \leqslant i \leqslant k-1$ and $a_0 = 1, 3, 5, 7$ or 9. Then

$$n^2 = (a_k 10^k + \ldots + a_1 10 + a_0)^2$$
$$= N \cdot 10^2 + 2a_0 a_1 \cdot 10 + a_0^2, \quad \text{where } N \text{ is an integer.}$$

Now $a_0^2 = 1 \ (= 01)$, $9 \ (= 09)$, 25, 49 or 81 and so has an even tens digit. Also $2a_0 a_1$ has an even remainder on division by 10. From these facts the result follows. Note that the units digit for n^2 is 1, 5 or 9.

(10) A test for divisibility by 19 is provided by the following rule. From the number to be tested remove the last digit (units digit) and add to the number remaining twice the digit crossed off. Continue this process; e.g.

$$308655 \to 30865 + 10 = 30875$$
$$30875 \to 3087 + 10 = 3097$$
$$3097 \to 309 + 14 = 323$$
$$323 \to 32 + 6 = 38$$
$$38 \to 3 + 16 = 19$$

Hence 308655 is divisible by 19; check this. Try to justify the rule. Generalize this rule for division by 21 (7), 29, 31, ... (See Kashangaki, *Mathematical Gazette* 41, p. 122 (1957).)

(11) *Palindromes.* A palindrome is a positive integer whose decimal digits read the same backwards as forwards; e.g. 22, 1331, 935686539.

How many 2-digit palindromes are there?

How many 3-digit palindromes are there?

How many k-digit palindromes are there?

Prove that every 4-digit palindrome is divisible by 11. Is the same true for 6-digit palindromes?

Take a 2-digit number, reverse it, add this to the original. Is the result a palindrome? If not, repeat the process. It is found that all 2-digit numbers lead to palindromes in this way after a few steps. Which 2-digit number takes the most steps? (89 takes 24 steps.)

Experiment with 3-digit numbers using the same process.

(12) Carry out a project on *recurring decimals*, using suitable books to begin your investigations.

(13) Carry out a project on *continued fractions*, using suitable books-to begin your investigations. In particular, by taking the decimal expansion of π to enough places, obtain the continued fraction

$$\pi = 3 + \frac{1}{7+} \frac{1}{15+} \frac{1}{1+} \cdots,$$

and explain why $\frac{22}{7}, \frac{333}{106}, \frac{355}{113}$ are "good" approximations to π.

(14) The numbers 0, 5, 76, 625 have squares 0, 25, 5776, 390625, which end in the numbers themselves; e.g. $76^2 = 5776$, which ends in 76. Determine all 1-digit, 2-digit, 3-digit and 4-digit such numbers.

(15) Investigate the sequence of results:

$$121_3 = 4^2, \quad 121_4 = 5^2, \quad 121_5 = 6^2, \ldots.$$

Conjecture a result and try to prove it. Can you discover other results of the same kind? Evaluate 169_b in base 10 for $b \geqslant 10$.

(16) The first four perfect numbers are $1 = 1$, $6 = 1+2+3$, $28 = 1+2+4+7+14$, $496 = 1+2+4+8+16+31+62+124+248$. Divide each in turn by 1, 6, 28 and 496 respectively; e.g. $1 = \frac{1}{6}+\frac{1}{3}+\frac{1}{2}$. Investigate what happens when each fraction is expressed in binary notation (i.e. as an expansion in base 2).

(17) *A number game* (using the following tables)

Table 1				Table 2				Table 4			
1	9	17	25	2	10	18	26	4	12	20	28
3	11	19	27	3	11	19	27	5	13	21	29
5	13	21	29	6	14	22	30	6	14	22	30
7	15	23	31	7	15	23	31	7	15	23	31

Table 8				Table 16			
8	12	24	28	16	20	24	28
9	13	25	29	17	21	25	29
10	14	26	30	18	22	26	30
11	15	27	31	19	23	27	31

Pick a number at random from 1 to 31 and check which of the five tables it appears in. What happens if you add the numbers of the tables in which your number appears? If the pupil cannot explain the result, his attention could be drawn to the number base suggested by the table numbers.

10.4. Problems Involving Prime and Composite Numbers

As in 10.3, we have produced with little comment or helpful suggestions a collection of problems that can be used to initiate pupil investigations. Some will require development.

(An integer $p > 1$ is a *prime number* if 1 and p are its only positive divisors; every other integer > 1 is said to be *composite*.)

(1) Use the sieve of Eratosthenes to find all the primes < 500.

(2) A prime (number) of the form

$$2^p - 1$$

where p itself is a prime, is called a *Mersenne* prime. Investigate these for $p = 2, 3, 5, 7, \ldots$ as far as you can by hand or by calculator. At present 24 such primes are known, the largest of these,

$$2^{19937} - 1$$

being discovered by computer in 1971. Investigate the representation of these primes in binary notation.

It is known that an *even perfect number* is of the form $2^{p-1}(2^p-1)$, where 2^p-1 is a Mersenne prime, so that 24 even perfect numbers are at present known. (It is not known whether an *odd* perfect number exists.) Check this as far as you can. Deduce that an even perfect number is a triangular number.

(3) A prime of the form

$$2^{2^r}+1$$

is called a *Fermat prime*. Fermat conjectured that every number of this type is a prime, but the only primes so far discovered are those for $r = 0, 1, 2, 3$ and 4. Check these as far as you can.

(4) Verify that $x^2 - x + 41$ is prime for $0 \leqslant x < 41$ but not for $x = 41$. Verify that $x^2 - 79x + 1601 = (x-40)^2 + (x-40) + 41$ is prime for $0 \leqslant x \leqslant 79$ but not for $x = 80$. (Since this can also be written as $(x-39)^2 - (x-39) + 41$, it can be deduced from the first part.) Try to discover other similar results.

(5) Investigate for $1 \leqslant n \leqslant 50$ when $n^2 + 1$ is prime and, if composite, find all its factors. (It is an unsolved conjecture that the set of primes of the form $n^2 + 1$ is infinite.)

(6) Find integers n for which

(a) $n+1, n+2$ and $n+3$ are all composite,

(b) $n+1, n+2, n+3$ and $n+4$ are all composite,

(c) $n+1, n+2, n+3, n+4$ and $n+5$ are all composite.

(7) Find numbers of the form $11, 111, 1111, 11111, \ldots$; i.e. whose digits are all 1, which are prime $((10^{23}-1)/9$ is one of these), and factorize the others. It is not known whether the set of such primes is infinite.

(8) *Twin primes*. Primes of the form $p, p+2$, i.e. differing by 2, are called twin primes. Find all such twins up to as large as possible a value of p. Show that, for $p \geqslant 5$, all such twins can be expressed in the form $6k-1, 6k+1$. It is an unsolved conjecture that the set of prime twins is infinite. Find a sequence of integers of the form

$$6k-1, 6k+1, 6k+5, 6k+7, 6k+11, 6k+13, \ldots$$

as long as you possibly can, all of which are primes.

(9) *Goldbach's conjecture.* This famous unsolved conjecture says that every *even* positive integer $\geqslant 4$ can be expressed as the sum of two primes. Verify it for all even integers n satisfying $4 \leqslant n \leqslant 100$ (or more). What similar result would you expect to hold for *odd* integers $\geqslant 9$ which are not primes?

(10) Determine for positive integers $n \leqslant 100$ those for which each of n and $n+1$ has only one prime divisor (e.g. $n = 2, 3, 4, 7, \ldots$). It is an unsolved problem as to whether the set of all such n is infinite.

(11) (i) Tartaglia in 1556 claimed that the sums

$$1+2+4, 1+2+4+8, 1+2+4+8+16$$

are alternately prime and composite. Show that he was wrong.

(ii) De Bouvelles in 1509 stated that one or both of $6k-1$ and $6k+1$ (k a positive integer) are prime for all k. Show that he was also wrong.

(12) If the set of primes in increasing order of magnitude is $\{p_1, p_2, p_3, \ldots\}$, find the first two values of n for which $p_1 p_2 \ldots p_n + 1$ is composite.

(13) Discuss the existence of squares in the sets

$$\{3p+1 : p \text{ a prime}\}, \{3p+2 : p \text{ a prime}\},$$

$$\{5p+1 : p \text{ a prime}\}, \{5p+2 : p \text{ a prime}\}.$$

(14) Investigate the set $\{p^2 + 2 : p \text{ a prime} \geqslant 5\}$. Make a conjecture about primes in the set and try to prove it.

(15) It seems unusual for the sum of the proper divisors of an odd number to be even. Try to determine when this is the case. (Remember that 1 is counted as a proper divisor.) Let $n = p_1^{\alpha_1} \ldots p_r^{\alpha_r}$ be the prime factorization of n, so that $p_1, \ldots, p_r$ are distinct odd primes and each α_i is a positive integer. The set of all positive

divisors of n is

$$D = \{p_1^{\beta_1}, \ldots, p_r^{\beta_r} : 0 \leqslant \beta_i \leqslant \alpha_i \quad (i = 1, \ldots, r)\}$$

and the set of all *proper* divisors of n is $D - \{n\}$.

The *sum* of the proper divisors of n is

$$(1 + p_1 + p_1^2 + \ldots + p_1^{\alpha_1})(1 + p_2 + p_2^2 + \ldots + p_2^{\alpha_2}) \ldots$$
$$(1 + p_r + p_r^2 + \ldots + p_r^{\alpha_r}) - n.$$

Thus this sum is *even*

$\Leftrightarrow (1 + p_1 + \ldots + p_1^{\alpha_1})(1 + p_2 + \ldots + p_2^{\alpha_2}) \ldots (1 + p_r + \ldots + p_r^{\alpha_r})$ is odd

$\Leftrightarrow$ each factor is *odd*

$\Leftrightarrow$ the number of terms in each factor is *odd*

$\Leftrightarrow$ each α_i is *even*.

(16) Produce chains of numbers as follows:

Start with a positive integer and produce a chain of numbers with the property that each is the sum of the proper divisors of its predecessor; e.g.

```
20 → 1+2+4+5+10 = 22
22 → 1+2+11       = 14
14 → 1+2+7        = 10
10 → 1+2+5        = 8
8 → 1+2+4         = 7
7 → 1
```

A *perfect number* is a chain of length 1. *Amicable numbers* are numbers connected by chains of length 2 (e.g. 1184, 1210; 2620, 2964). Investigate these.

(17) By finding suitable counter-examples, show that the following statements about positive integers are false:

(a) If $a|m$ and $b|m$, then $ab|m$.

(b) If $a|mn$, then either $a|m$ or $a|n$.

(c) If p is prime, $p|a$ and $p|(a^2 + 3b^2)$, then $p|b$.

(d) If p is prime, $p|(a^2 + b^2)$ and $p|(b^2 + c^2)$, then $p|(a^2 + c^2)$.

(18) List all of the primes < 200 in the following arithmetic progressions:

(a) $\{4n + 1 : n = 0, 1, 2, \ldots\}$,
(b) $\{12n + 7 : n = 0, 1, 2, \ldots\}$,
(c) $\{6n + 3 : n = 0, 1, 2, \ldots\}$,
(d) $\{6n + 4 : n = 0, 1, 2, \ldots\}$.

Dirichlet's theorem says that every arithmetic progression of the form $\{an + b : n = 0, 1, 2, \ldots\}$ where a and b are relatively prime integers (i.e. positive integers with no common factor > 1) contains an infinite number of primes. Determine exact results for (c) and (d).

(19) S is the set of integers $\{4k + 1 : k = 0, 1, 2, \ldots\}$ $= \{1, 5, 9, 13, \ldots\}$. An integer n (>1) in S is called an *S-prime* if 1 and n are the only factors of n in S. Draw up a list of S-primes. Show that factorization *in S* is not unique by showing that 441 is the smallest integer in S that can be expressed in two different ways as a product of S-primes. Find the next such integer.

(20) For the set $E = \{2, 4, 6, 8, 10, \ldots\}$ define an *E-prime*, and verify that factorization *in E* as a product of *E-primes* is not necessarily unique.

10.5. Diophantine Equations and Representation Problems

(This work involves looking for solutions of equations in integers. The word Diophantine is derived from the name of Diophantus of Alexandria who lived in the third century AD and was one of the first to make a study of equations in integers.)

Some of the following problems could be used for pupil investigations or be developed for classroom activities.

(1) *Pythagorean triples.* These are triples (x, y, z) of positive integers satisfying the Diophantine equation

$$x^2 + y^2 = z^2 \tag{1}$$

What is the obvious connection with the theorem of Pythagoras?

Find all the Pythagorean triples involving integers < 100. (By symmetry, we can regard $(3, 4, 5)$ as "essentially the same" as $(4, 3, 5)$.) Find Pythagorean triangles whose areas are numerically equal to their perimeters (e.g. that given by triple $(5, 12, 13)$). It can be shown that the solutions of (1) with no common factor are given by the equations

$$x = a^2 - b^2, \quad y = 2ab, \quad z = a^2 + b^2$$

where a, b are integers with $a > b > 0$ with no common factor, and not both odd; e.g.

$a = 2, b = 1$ gives the triple $(3, 4, 5)$

$a = 3, b = 2$ gives the triple $(5, 12, 13)$.

Verify this result for some of the triples that you have obtained.

(2) *Fermat's last theorem.* Fermat stated that all the Diophantine equations

$$x^n + y^n = z^n$$

for integers $n \geqslant 3$ have no solutions, except when at least one of x, y is zero. We still do not know whether this statement is true or false, but, in trying to prove it, many contributions have been made to mathematics. Examine the trivial cases when at least one of x, y is zero. Find out what you can about our present knowledge on the problem.

(3) Consider the Diophantine equation

$$x^2 - y^2 = n$$

Taking squares of integers x, y with $x > y \geqslant 0$ and forming $x^2 - y^2$, convince yourself that the equation has solutions if and only if n is odd or divisible by 4. Can you find simple solutions when $n = 2k + 1$ and when $n = 4k$, where k is a given positive integer?

(4) An unsolved problem is whether the set of equations

$$\{y^2 = x^3 + p : p \text{ a prime}\}$$

has an infinite subset with *no* solutions (e.g. $y^2 = x^3 + 7$ has no integer solutions (positive or negative); it is not easy to prove this!). Consider some of these equations for given primes p and look for solutions.

(5) The Diophantine equation

$$\frac{1}{x} + \frac{1}{y} = \frac{1}{6}$$

has 17 solutions in integers, positive or negative. Find them. Similarly find the 13 solutions of the equation

$$\frac{1}{x} + \frac{1}{y} = \frac{1}{8}.$$

(6) Four solutions in ("small") integers, positive or negative, are known of the Diophantine equation

$$x^3 + y^3 + z^3 = 3.$$

Find them. It is not known if these are all the solutions.

(7) An unsolved conjecture is that the Diophantine equation

$$\frac{1}{x} + \frac{1}{y} + \frac{1}{z} = \frac{4}{n}$$

has solutions in x, y, z for each given integer $n > 1$. Verify the result for some values of n.

(8) Explore for solutions of the Diophantine equation

$$3^x - 2^y = 1$$

taking integral values of x, y in the range 1 to 10 with $x \neq y$. Verify that you get one such solution; it can be shown (not too easily!) that this is the only solution of the equation. In fact it is an unproved conjecture that no two consecutive integers, except 8 and 9, are composite perfect powers.

(9) It is a known fact that every positive integer can be expressed as a sum of 1, 2, 3 or 4 squares of positive integers. Express all the

integers from 1 to 100 as sums of such squares. Clearly perfect squares require one square. Otherwise the following results hold:

(i) n ($\geqslant 1$) can be expressed as $x^2 + y^2$ when any prime divisors of n of the form $4k+3$ (e.g. 3, 7, ...) appear to an even power (all other prime divisors are either 2 or of the form $4k+1$);

(ii) n ($\geqslant 1$) can be expressed as $x^2 + y^2 + z^2$ unless n is of the form $4^r(8k+7)$ for some r and k, when four squares are needed.

(In (i) and (ii) the square 0^2 may appear.) Verify the results (i) and (ii) for the work that you did with the integers $n = 1$ to $n = 100$. In particular check the form of the 15 integers that require four squares. Which of the integers 1977, 1978, 1979, 1980, 1981, 1982, 1983 can be expressed as a sum of two squares? If n is the sum of two triangular numbers, then $4n+1$ is a sum of two squares. Verify this in a number of cases and try to prove it in general.

(10) Investigate expressing numbers n as sums of cubes

$$11 = 2^3 + 1^3 + 1^3 + 1^3$$
$$73 = 4^3 + 2^3 + 1^3.$$

Consider $n = 1$ to $n = 300$ (or more). Which numbers need most cubes? 23 and 239 need 9 cubes and are thought to be the only integers requiring more than 8 cubes.

(11) *Use of the integer lattice for Diophantine equations*

Use of circles. Since the circle with centre the origin and radius r has equation $x^2 + y^2 = r^2$, we can use circles with radii $\sqrt{n}$ ($n = 1, 2, 3, ...$) to investigate those integers n for which $n = x^2 + y^2$ with x and y integers. Also we can determine the number of such representations for each n. Carry out a geometrical investigation of this type.

Use of the integer lattice for an approximation to π. Locate the point A $(\sqrt{2}, \frac{1}{3})$ in the x, y plane. Using compasses (or a ruler) check that the points of the integer lattice can be named $P_1, P_2, P_3, ...$ in such a way that $|AP_1| < |AP_2| < |AP_3| < ...$, where $|AP|$ denotes the distance from A to P. Then the circle with

centre A and radius $|AP_{n+1}|$ contains exactly n of the points of the integer lattice inside it, namely $P_1, ..., P_n$. Shade in the n unit squares with centres $P_1, ..., P_n$ and sides parallel to the axes, giving

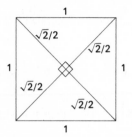

a region of area n. If $r = |AP_{n+1}|$, check that this region contains the circle with centre A and radius $r - \sqrt{2}/2$ but is contained in the circle with centre A and radius $r + \sqrt{2}/2$. From this sandwich effect we deduce:

$$\frac{n}{(r+\sqrt{2}/2)^2} \leqslant \pi \leqslant \frac{n}{(r-\sqrt{2}/2)^2}$$

By choosing a suitably large value of n and measuring $r = |AP_{n+1}|$ and by taking an appropriate approximate value for $\sqrt{2}$, obtain inequalities for π.

10.6. Problems on Modular Arithmetic and Some Other Topics

This work can be recommended only for able pupils and on the whole leads to post-"O" Level activities.

$a \equiv b \pmod{m}$ means $m|(a-b)$, i.e. $a - b = km$ for some integer k, i.e. m divides $a-b$, i.e. a and b have the same remainder on division by m.

At whatever stage this sort of work is introduced it is important to have a feeling for division, quotients and remainders. Dividing integer a by positive integer b means

$$a = qb + r, \; q \text{ and } r \text{ integers with } 0 \leqslant r < b.$$

Then

$$\frac{a}{b} = q + \frac{r}{b} \quad \text{with} \quad 0 \leqslant \frac{r}{b} < 1.$$

Thus the quotient q is $\left[\dfrac{a}{b}\right]$, the *integral part* of $\dfrac{a}{b}$, i.e. the unique integer q such that $q \leqslant \dfrac{a}{b} < q+1$.

(1) *Integral part function.* ($[x]$, the integral part of real number x, is the integer nearest to x from below; $[x] \leqslant x < [x]+1$; $x = [x]+t$ where $0 \leqslant t < 1$; e.g. $[3] = 3$, $[-2\frac{1}{2}] = -3$, $[\pi] = 3$, etc.)

Why is the graph of $[x]$ an infinite step ladder?

What is $[x+\frac{1}{2}]$?

Verify the following for some real numbers or try to prove the results:

(a) $[x+n] = [x]+n$, where n is an integer.

(b) $[x]+[-x] = 0$ when x is an integer and -1 otherwise.

(c) $[x+y] \geqslant [x]+[y]$.

(d) $\left[\dfrac{n+1}{2}\right] + \left[\dfrac{n+2}{2^2}\right] + \left[\dfrac{n+2^2}{2^3}\right] + \ldots = ?$, where n is a positive integer, determining the correct replacement for "?". (The binary representation of n will help in proving this.)

(2) Consider the powers of 7. What is the remainder when they are divided by 6? Is this surprising?

(3) Complete the following table:

$a \equiv 0$	1	2	3	4	5	6	(mod 7)
$a^2 \equiv 0$	1	2	3	4	5	6	(mod 7)
$a^3 \equiv$							
$a^4 \equiv$							
$a^5 \equiv$							
$a^6 \equiv$							

If a is prime to 7 there is a least positive integer r such that $a^r \equiv 1 \pmod{7}$; r is called the *order of a* (mod 7). What are the orders (mod 7) of 1, 2, 3, 4, 5 and 6?

How many of the possible remainders $0, 1, 2, 3, 4, 5, 6, 7$ on division by 8 are prime to 8? Find the order of these integers (mod 8). Deduce that, if a is odd, then $8|(a^2-1)$.

If m is a given positive integer, the number of integers in the set $\{1, 2, \ldots, m\}$, or the set $\{0, 1, \ldots, m-1\}$ if $m > 1$, that are prime to m, is denoted by $\phi(m)$, where ϕ is called *Euler's function*. Find $\phi(m)$ for $m = 1, \ldots, 20$. What is the value of $\phi(p)$ where p is a prime? It can be shown that, if a is prime to m, then

$$a^{\phi(m)} \equiv 1 \pmod{m}.$$

Verify this in a number of cases. It can also be shown that, if p is a prime, then

$$a^p - a \equiv 0 \pmod{p} \text{ for every integer } a.$$

Verify this in a number of cases.

Verify the following in some cases (each holds for every integer a):

(i) $a^3 - a \equiv 0 \pmod{6}$,

(ii) $a^5 - a \equiv 0 \pmod{10}$,

(iii) $a^7 - a \equiv 0 \pmod{42}$.

(4) By considering suitable squares (mod 10), show that no square has as its last digit 2, 3, 7 or 8.

(5) Think of an *even* number. Multiply it by the next number;

then multiply this product by the next number again (e.g. $8 \times 9 \times 10 = ?$). Is the answer divisible by 24? If you think that the answer is always divisible by 24, try to prove the result.

(6) Consider numbers of the form $4^n + 6n - 1$, where n is a positive integer. Are they multiples of 9? If you think they are always divisible by 9, try to prove the result.

(7) Test the following result for various values of m: "The product of the positive integers $< m$ and prime to m is $\equiv -1 \pmod{m}$ when $m = 4$, p^r or $2p^r$ (p an odd prime) and $\equiv 1 \pmod{m}$ in every other case".

(8) List integers n such that

$$n \equiv 1 \pmod 2$$

and

$$n \equiv 2 \pmod 3.$$

Can you make a conjecture about the set of all integers n which satisfy these two relations?

(9) Test the following result for various values of n: "Every integer $n > 0$ satisfies at least one of

$$n \equiv 0 \pmod 2, \quad n \equiv 0 \pmod 3, \quad n \equiv 1 \pmod 4,$$
$$n \equiv 3 \pmod 8, \quad n \equiv 7 \pmod{12}, \quad n \equiv 23 \pmod{24}".$$

Such a system is called a *covering system of congruences*.

10.7. Background to Number Theory

At some stage of his development a pupil with ability and interest in mathematics may well raise questions about how some of the many results and facts listed in sections 1 to 6 of this chapter can be proved. We recognize that, when working with pupils on this material, the word "proof" should not imply too formal a meaning, especially in the earlier years; it is more important to try to capture interest and "imagination" with the type of "imaginative thinking" presented. However, many teachers, who have not had any formal training in number theory, may wish to have information about the background material that is needed to provide proofs of the results and in particular to have suitable references.

As was stated on page 15, elementary number theory deals with properties of the positive integers and arises essentially from the consequences of the division identity for Z, the set of all integers, namely, that, if a, b are integers, with $b > 0$, then there exist unique integers q and r such that

$$a = qb + r \quad \text{and} \quad 0 \leqslant r < b.$$

From this result, it follows that

$$\frac{a}{b} = q + \frac{r}{b} \quad \text{and} \quad 0 \leqslant \frac{r}{b} < 1$$

so that $q = [a/b]$, the integral part of the rational number a/b. This latter fact highlights the important fact about number theory, that, to obtain properties of the set N, it may be necessary to work in an extension of N such as W, Z, Q, R or C.

As background to the development of number theory, we need the usual properties of decimal representation, addition, subtraction, multiplication, division and ordering for the integers (or appropriate extensions), basic algebra such as index laws, binomial expansions and simple summations, and the important principle of induction. Some of the results given in this chapter can be proved with only the amount of information so far listed, but with possibly a fair amount of ingenuity.

Consider first property (iv) of the hexagonal numbers H_n (see p. 98), i.e. that the end digits of H_n ($n = 1, 2, 3, \ldots$) occur cyclically in the order 1, 7, 9, 7, 1.

Proof. $H_n = 3n^2 - 3n + 1 \qquad (n = 1, 2, 3, \ldots).$

Since we are concerned only with the end digits we can use the table:

| n: | 1 | 2 | 3 | 4 | 5 | 6 | 7 | 8 | 9 | 0, |

since $n = 11, 12, \ldots$ gives cyclic repetition of these ten digits. We can complete the table:

n:	1	2	3	4	5	6	7	8	9	0
$-3n$:	-3	-6	-9	-12	-15	-18	-21	-24	-27	0
n^2:	1	4	9	16	25	36	49	64	81	0
$3n^2$:	3	12	27	48	75	108	147	192	243	0
$3n^2 - 3n + 1$:	1	7	9	7	1	1	7	9	7	1

where, in the last row, only the end digit has been recorded. This proves the result.

Let us now consider problem 6 of Section 10.6 (p. 113); we show that $4^n + 6n - 1$ is divisible by 9 for each integer $n \geqslant 1$.

Proof (by induction)

The result is easily checked for $n = 1$. Assume that the statement is true for $n = k \ (\geqslant 1)$ so that

$$4^k + 6k - 1 = 9N, \quad \text{for some integer } N.$$

Then $4^{k+1} + 6(k+1) - 1 = 4(9N - 6k + 1) + 6k + 5 = 9(4N - 2k + 1)$, and so the statement involved is also true for $n = k + 1$.

The result now follows by induction.

The next stage in building up background to number theory is to study the immediate consequences of the division identity for Z. These are presented in chapter 6 (pages 86–116) of *Algebra and Number Systems* by J. Hunter *et al.* (Blackie/Chambers); in fact this book could in many senses be regarded as a "follow-up" to the present book on *Number*. The sequence of topics discussed is:

(1) the division identity, integral and fractional parts,
(2) number bases (justification for expressing integers to base g),
(3) l.c.m., g.c.d. (or H.C.F.), euclidean algorithm,
(4) prime numbers, unique prime factorization (i.e. fundamental theorem of arithmetic) (statement of prime number theorem, some unsolved problems),

(5) congruence notation, some results on congruences up to:

$$(a, m) = 1 \Rightarrow a^{\phi(m)} \equiv 1 \ (\text{mod } m),$$

where ϕ is Euler's function (see example 23, p. 116 of Hunter's book).

The chapter contains many examples and there are further examples in the two additional sets of examples at the end of the book.

This body of work gives us enough background to provide proofs for many of the results listed. We consider a few of these.

Section 10.6, *Problem* 1 (*d*) (page 112): Show that, for all $n \in N$,

$$\left[\frac{n+1}{2}\right] + \left[\frac{n+2}{2^2}\right] + \left[\frac{n+2^2}{2^3}\right] + \ldots = n. \tag{1}$$

Proof. Express n in base 2; say

$$n = 2^k + a_{k-1}2^{k-1} + \ldots + a_2 2^2 + a_1 2 + a_0$$

where each $a_i = 0$ or 1.

$$\left[\frac{n+1}{2}\right] = 2^{k-1} + a_{k-1}2^{k-2} + \ldots + a_3 2^2 + a_2 2 + a_1 + \left[\frac{a_0 + 1}{2}\right]$$

$$= 2^{k-1} + \ldots + a_1 + a_0$$

since $\left[\dfrac{a_0 + 1}{2}\right] = 0$ when $a_0 = 0$ and $\left[\dfrac{a_0 + 1}{2}\right] = 1$ when $a_0 = 1$.

In this way, the left-hand side of (1) is

$$\begin{aligned}
&2^{k-1} + a_{k-1}2^{k-2} + \ldots + a_3 2^2 + a_2 2 + a_1 + a_0 \\
&+ 2^{k-2} + a_{k-1}2^{k-3} + \ldots + a_3 2 + a_2 + a_1 \\
&+ 2^{k-3} + a_{k-1}2^{k-4} + \ldots + a_3 + a_2 \\
&+ \ldots \\
&+ 2 + a_{k-1} + a_{k-2} \\
&+ 1 + a_{k-1} \\
&+ 1 \\
&+ 0 \\
&= 2^k + a_{k-1}2^{k-1} + \ldots + a_3 2^3 + a_2 2^2 + a_1 2 + a_0 = n.
\end{aligned}$$

Section 10.6, *Problem* 5 (page 112): Think of an even number. Multiply it by the next two numbers and show that the product is always divisible by 24.

Proof. We have to show that $24|2k(2k+1)(2k+2)$, where k is a positive integer.

Since $2k$, $2k+1$, $2k+2$ are consecutive integers, one of them is divisible by 3 (and the other two have remainders 1 and 2 on division by 3). Thus

$$3|2k(2k+1)(2k+2)$$

The result will follow if we now show that

$$8|2k(2k+1)(2k+2),$$

since 3 and 8 are prime to each other. Now

$$2k(2k+1)(2k+2) = 4k(k+1)(2k+1)$$

$$= 8 \times \text{an integer}$$

since either k or $k+1$ is even.

The result now follows.

Section 10.6, *Problem* 8 (page 113): Find the general solution of the system of congruences

$$n \equiv 1 \,(\mathrm{mod}\,2),$$

$$n \equiv 2 \,(\mathrm{mod}\,3).$$

One solution is $n = 5$, and the system is equivalent to

$$n \equiv 5 \,(\mathrm{mod}\,2), \quad n \equiv 5 \,(\mathrm{mod}\,3).$$

Clearly these hold if and only if $n \equiv 5 \,(\mathrm{mod}\,6)$, and the solution set is $\{6u + 5 : u \in Z\}$.

In the Introduction, the problem was raised of showing that $7|(5555^{2222} + 2222^{5555})$. We can prove this as follows:

$$\phi(7) = 6; \quad (a, 7) = 1 \Rightarrow a^6 \equiv 1 \,(\mathrm{mod}\,7).$$

Now $(5555, 7) = 1$ and $(2222, 7) = 1$ and $2222 \equiv 2 \,(\mathrm{mod}\,6)$ and $5555 \equiv 5 \,(\mathrm{mod}\,6)$; thus

$$5555^{2222} + 2222^{5555} \equiv 5555^2 + 2222^5 \,(\mathrm{mod}\,7)$$

$$\equiv 4^2 + 3^5 \,(\mathrm{mod}\,7)$$

$$= 259 \equiv 0 \,(\mathrm{mod}\,7).$$

Hence the result is true.

Our final proof is harder, requiring a knowledge of quadratic residues which are referred to in H. Davenport, *The Higher Arithmetic*, chapter 3.

Section 10.6, *Problem* 7 (page 113): The product of the positive integers $< m$ and prime to m is $\equiv -1 \,(\mathrm{mod}\,m)$ when $m = 4$, p^r or $2p^r$ (p an odd prime).

Proof. When $m = 4$, p^r or $2p^r$, m has a primitive root, g say. Then $\{1 = g^0, g, g^2, \ldots, g^{\phi(m)-1}\}$ is a reduced set of residues (mod m) and so is congruent to the set of integers $< m$ and prime to m. It follows that the product of the integers $< m$ and prime to m is

$$\equiv g^{0+1+2+\ldots+(\phi(m)-1)} \,(\mathrm{mod}\,m)$$

$$\equiv (g^{\phi(m)/2})^{\phi(m)-1}, \text{ noting that } \phi(m) \text{ is even,}$$

$$\equiv (-1)^{\phi(m)-1} \,(\mathrm{mod}\,m)$$

$$\equiv -1 \,(\mathrm{mod}\,m).$$

We hope that this brief survey of some background work in number theory may stimulate the reader who has not yet met the subject or who would like to refresh previous knowledge.

10.8. Summary

This chapter has covered a very wide range of topics in number and, although some of the problems have been difficult, many of them have been suitable for investigation by pupils of wide-ranging abilities. It has been repeatedly made clear that in many cases development of problems will be needed for general class-room use. This has not been done, partly because the work involved would be enormous and would require a book much larger than this one, but also because there are often many different ways in which problems can be developed.

References

H. Davenport, *The Higher Arithmetic: an introduction to the theory of numbers* (Hutchinson, 1970).

G. H. Hardy and E. M. Wright, *Introduction to the Theory of Numbers* (OUP, 1960)

C. S. Banwell, K. D. Saunders and D. G. Tahta. *Starting Points for Teaching Mathematics in Middle and Secondary Schools* (OUP, 1972)

A. J. Moakes, P. D. Croome and T. C. Phillips, *Pattern and Power of Mathematics 1–6* (Macmillan, 1967–69)

C. S. Ogilvy and J. T. Anderson, *Excursions in Number Theory* (OUP, 1967)

J. Hunter *et al., Algebra and Number-Systems* (Blackie. 1971)

Appendix 1

Recommendations

(1) *Applications*

Computational skills on their own are useless skills. They need to be taught and practised regularly in the context of simple applications.

(2) *Measurement*

The skills of measurement and ideas of accuracy should be learnt in mathematics lessons. These skills will be used and reinforced in other subject lessons (e.g. home economics, geography and chemistry).

(3) *Practice in arithmetic*

Arithmetical skills are best acquired and maintained in a rich context. Statistics projects, computing projects and investigations in number theory and combinatorics can all be used to give regular practice in areas which both demand and reward these skills. (Examples may be found in *Mathematics in the World* and *Counting and Configurations*, books in this series, as well as in chapter 10 of the present book.)

SOME SPECIFIC POINTS

(4) *The understanding of place value*

The understanding of place value is crucial for the learning of computational skills. Meaningless calculations in multibase arithmetic do little to improve the understanding of children who find difficulty with the concept of place value; indeed, the main purpose of such calculations is to help clarify the concept, and they are meaningful only if they fulfil that purpose.

(5) *Fractions*

Fractions appear in various ways and should be recognized as parts of a whole, as "shares" (e.g. 3 divided by 7) and as expressions of ratios. The first two aspects should be understood, together with the ideas of equivalent fractions and ordering, before formal methods with the four rules are attempted.

(6) *Decimal fractions*

The effect of multiplying and dividing by powers of ten should be emphasized, and there should be regular practice in measurements involving decimals and in the reading of number scales generally.

A CORE SYLLABUS

(7) Basic arithmetic. Four rules. Squares. Tables.

Representation of numbers on a number-line.

Powers of ten. Place value.

Units of measurement. Areas and volumes.

Ratio and proportion.

Concentrations, mixtures, percentages.

Orders of magnitudes, estimation, approximate checks.

Organization of calculation. Flow diagrams.

Fractions and decimals (four rules).

Graphical representation of data and relations.

Square roots.

Elementary statistical calculations.

Social arithmetic.

Experience of a variety of calculating aids.

FURTHER POINTS

(8) The number systems (N, Z, Q, R) should be appreciated in order to recognize what sort of solution is expected to a problem and, with some pupils, to illustrate the development of mathematics. The connections with geometry and algebra are particularly fruitful here.

(9) Children should appreciate which computing aids are best suited to particular calculations.

Appendix 2

Extracts from "Report of a Conference on the Teaching of Arithmetic in London Elementary Schools Dec. 1906–Dec. 1908"

(This conference was convened in 1906; the proceedings were published in 1911 by London County Council Education Committee, and reprinted in 1914 and 1923. The report appears to be mainly the work of B. Branford, the conference chairman, and LCC divisional inspector.)

At such a time the urgency of the need of taking counsel together in conference is equalled only by the difficulty of the task encountered.

The object of the conference was three-fold. To search out the essential contributions of the past: to recognise the incipient developments of the future: and to discover, if may be, a middle course by which the former may be retained and the latter encouraged to grow, by a careful survey of the actual state of the present. (General Introduction, p. 9)

Still rarer is it to find the mathematical work effectively correlated with science, geography and manual or domestic work; though a carefully considered treatment of these should offer many interesting, valuable and simple applications of arithmetical and geometrical principles. Moreover, *many of the problems presented in these adjacent fields of school work might with great advantage serve from time to time as points of departure for the stimulation and development of underlying mathematical ideas which could be worked out in the mathematical classroom.* (Chapter 1, §3(d), p. 20) (italics original)

In teaching Arithmetic a twofold aim must be kept in view. On the one hand the intelligence of the pupils must be developed, and on the other hand they must be made practically skillful in the subject for the ordinary purposes of life. Not only is each of these ends valuable in itself, but their relation to one another and their reaction upon one another are such as to make it necessary that both should be constantly borne in mind. Practice in Arithmetical operations and the acquirement of skill in performing them are essential to the full apprehension of them, while on the other hand only a very low standard of practical skill can be attained if the development of the intelligence is neglected. The aim of Arithmetic teaching, then, may be said to be to lead the scholars

(i) to "think clearly and systematically about number" and to acquire the power of doing this by dealing with the objects and ideas presented to them in their everyday life;

(ii) to acquire a reasonable degree of automatic skill in the use of the machinery, i.e., in the use of Arithmetical operations and their various combinations.

It necessarily follows from what has been said above that part of the purpose of Arithmetic teaching should be to lead the pupils to apply their knowledge and skill to the practical problems of life.

In order that this twofold aim may be successfully carried out certain general considerations must be constantly borne in mind:

(i) the teaching should in the main be based upon the child's own experience and previous knowledge, and, especially in the earlier stages, upon definite experiments made by him with concrete objects. It is not enough that the teacher should perform these experiments in the presence of his class; each child should handle the objects himself and should for himself make such discoveries as are suitable to the stage he has reached.

(ii) Similarly axioms, definitions, formulations of rules and the formal expression of arguments should always follow and proceed from the children's own examination of individual cases and their own solution of individual problems. Thus, for example, the rule for the addition of fractions should be reached by the child as a comprehensive and final statement of the various methods of procedure discovered by himself, guided where necessary by the teacher, in cases of gradually increasing complexity, e.g.,

$$\tfrac{1}{2}+\tfrac{1}{4}, \quad \tfrac{3}{4}+\tfrac{1}{8}, \quad \tfrac{2}{3}+\tfrac{5}{12}.$$

In leading the children to reach in this way their own generalizations great care must be taken not to hasten them in the process; premature generalization destroys a large part of the value of that process. It may be laid down as a general principle that such generalizations should not be introduced until the children have sufficient knowledge to be able, under the guidance of the teacher, to formulate them for themselves.

(iii) The place and function of memory in Arithmetic need careful consideration. The axioms, definitions and formulated rules referred to in the previous paragraph should be remembered, not by being learned by rote, but through being constantly applied and intelligently grasped. On the other hand, certain results needed for further progress (e.g., addition and multiplication tables) should finally be systematically committed to memory. (Chapter 1, §4(a), pp. 22/23)

Experience shows that the ultimate test of the pupil's attainment of arithmetical progress and power at any stage is in his ability to apply the ideas and processes which have been, presumably, mastered at that stage. Further, the tests given, to be genuine, must be presented to the pupil, not in the carefully classified form and highly conventional language of the textbook, but as problems based on difficulties such as might arise in practical everyday life. Such problems have a reality and concreteness that are vital to deep interest in the average pupil. But the supposition that quantity, applied to concrete things in which the pupil has small interest, is more stimulating to thought than abstract number, is not correct. Such quantity is only quasi-concrete; the inevitable conventional setting ultimately destroys its main concreteness. This will not be misinterpreted—after what has preceded—as a plea for teaching arithmetic purely by means of problems in abstract numbers; but it is a plea for deriving the arithmetical illustrations from the children's actual or imaginative experience and not from departments of thought or work quite beyond their ken. (Chapter 1, §4(b), p. 24)

Not only is a concrete everyday problem the final test of mastery of each main stage of the work, but the very first step of the mathematical process should in general itself arise from the need of finding the solution of some simple practical difficulty, within the experience of the pupil or within his imagination, demanding arithmetical or other mathematical knowledge.

Mathematics itself, and, therefore, the mathematical lesson, tend to stagnation unless constantly refreshed by new sources of concrete interest; these sources provide the fittest and most effective stimulus to the arousal and maintenance of emotions, ideas, and imagination—the inner driving forces of human thought activity. These principles are now well recognised and applied in the kindergarten, the technical college, and the university, but have, broadly speaking, still to be fully realized in the intermediate and upper stages of school work, both elementary and secondary. (Chapter 1, §4(c), p. 25)

To develop individuality and character, the pupil must be trained to rely on himself. He should be trained to think clearly and systematically about number, and to express his conclusions in his own language. All rules should be the expression of what he has been led to discover, and should only be used for the purpose of memorizing his results. Rules should be brought to a minimum and clearness of their underlying principles to a maximum. Technical terms should not be used till the thing they designate is known. Symbols and contractions should be introduced only when the need for them is felt, and the value of them can be interpreted. (Chapter 1, §13, p. 38)

Bibliography

Association of Teachers of Mathematics, *Turning the Tables* (1972)

This is a collection of number situations for children in the primary or the lower secondary school, written by members of the East Midlands region of the ATM.

Association of Teachers of Mathematics, *Numbers Everywhere* (1972)

This is a collection of number situations for secondary children, written by members of the East Midlands region of the ATM.

Both the above pamphlets are available from ATM, Market Street Chambers, Nelson, Lancs.

C. S. Banwell, K. D. Saunders & D. G. Tahta, *Starting Points*, OUP (1972)

This book is a collection of suggestions for the teaching of mathematics. It contains comments and questions on ways of working in the classroom, suggestions for starting points from which mathematics can be made and a large reference section. It is described as a book "to be dipped into, not a comprehensive or consecutive account".

A. B. Bolt and M. E. Wardle (for SMP), *Communicating with a Computer*, CUP (1970)

This is a well-presented examination of the connection between desk calculators and computers.

T. Dantzig, *Number, the Language of Science*, Allen and Unwin (1947)

There are other books which attempt to teach mathematics through its history. This is an old and established favourite which is entirely concerned with the history of numbers.

H. Davenport, *The Higher Arithmetic*, Hutchinson University Library (4th ed. 1970)

This is an introductory account of the theory of numbers. Themes for discussion include factorization and the primes, congruences, quadratic residues, continued fractions, sums of squares, and Diophantine equations, all of which appear in the problems in chapter 10. The theorems and their proofs are profusely illustrated by numerical examples.

S. V. Fomin, *Number Systems*, Chicago (1974)

This pamphlet belongs to the series Popular Lectures in Mathematics and is translated from the Russian. It discusses the origins, properties and applications of various number systems in a popular way.

G. H. Hardy and E. M. Wright, *An Introduction to the Theory of Numbers*, OUP (1960)

This is a classic, and it is harder than Davenport since it is written in a more formal way. It is a necessary book for reference in any mathematical library.

J. Hunter *et al.*, *Algebra and Number Systems*, Blackie/Chambers (1971)

This book is a sequel to the series of books on *Modern Mathematics for Schools* written by the Scottish Mathematics Group to provide Ordinary and Higher Grade courses for the Scottish Certificate of Education, and covers in particular the work required for Paper I of the Scottish Sixth Year Studies Examination in Mathematics.

The topics covered are mathematical logic, sets and relations, mappings, number systems, induction, finite summation, permutations and selections, elementary number theory, complex numbers, matrices and algebraic structures (a chapter each on (i) group theory, (ii) rings, integral domains, fields).

A. J. Moakes, *Numerical Mathematics*, Macmillan (1963)

This is a book of exercises for computing with a desk (hand-operated) calculator. It is a guide to the calculator, and the exercises are devised to use the machine to stimulate mathematical thought. Some of the exercises would only be suitable for the sixth form.

C. S. Ogilvy and J. T. Anderson, *Excursions in Number Theory*, OUP (1967)

An elementary introduction to number theory. It contains an interesting chapter on Fibonacci numbers.

F. F. Potter, *The Teaching of Arithmetic*, Pitman (1936)

This book is a text for colleges of education and teachers, etc., and is reviewed in detail in section 2.2.

D. A. Quadling, *The Same but Different*, Mathematical Association, Bell (1969)

This is a survey for teachers of the notion of equivalence in the context of school mathematics.

W. W. Sawyer, *Vision in Elementary Mathematics*, Penguin (1964)

The first of a series of popular books on elementary mathematics primarily designed for inexperienced teachers and parents. Contains sections on most topics in arithmetic, including negative numbers, fractions, factors and divisibility. Bursting with stimulating ideas for making things simple.

Schools Council (Mathematics for the Majority), *Number Appreciation*, Chatto & Windus (1971)

This is one of a series of guides written by the Mathematics for the Majority Project which was set up to help teachers construct courses for pupils of average and below-average ability. It contains a pleasant collection of applications of number, including, for example, applications to music: "The grand piano investigation" (p. 90).

W. Sierpinski, *A Selection of Problems in the Theory of Numbers*, Pergamon (1964)

This book contains several of the problems contained in chapter 10, and a great many more. It is divided into three very unequal parts; the largest discusses 29 problems relating to prime numbers—solved and unsolved. There is a short section on "the borders of geometry and arithmetic" in which *Problem* 11 of page 111 is discussed, among others; and a final set of 100 elementary but difficult problems in arithmetic, mostly unsolved. For anyone who finds chapter 10 fascinating, this is a stimulating follow-up.

H. Steinhaus, *One Hundred Problems in Elementary Mathematics*, Pergamon (1963)

A valuable collection of stimulating problems, with solutions, requiring little beyond secondary-school mathematics. Several are on number and combinatorics.

D. Wheeler, *R is for Real*, Open University Press (1974)

R is for Real was written to form part of an Open University course aimed to help school teachers to include a study of real numbers in their syllabuses. It is an unconventional text in a field in which readable texts are few. Its conclusions are not, in general, presented as the results of formal proof. The reader is invited instead to deduce for himself the need for the real numbers and the properties which they must possess.

Textbooks for Pupils

B. Holland and P. Rees, *Maths Today*, Harrap (1975), *Midlands Mathematical Experiment*, Harrap (1969)

A. J. Moakes, P. D. Croome and T. C. Phillips, *Pattern and Power of Mathematics*, Macmillan (1969)

G. W. Palmer, *Arithmetic*, Macmillan (1907)

Scottish Mathematics Group, *Modern Mathematics for Schools*, Books *1–7*, Blackie/Chambers (1971)

School Mathematics Project, *Books A–H, X–Z, 1–5*, CUP (1969–72)

Index